MW00748523

The WAY BACK

A Christian's Journey
to Mental Wholeness

The WAY BACK

DEACON ANDERSON AND ROBERT C. RICHARD, Ph.D.

WORD PUBLISHING
Dallas · London · Sydney · Singapore

THE WAY BACK: A CHRISTIAN'S JOURNEY TO MENTAL WHOLENESS

Copyright © 1989 by Deacon Anderson and Robert C. Richard.

All rights reserved. No portion of this book may be reproduced in any form, except for brief quotations in reviews, without written permission from the publisher.

Scripture quotations used in this book are from the following sources: The King James Version of the Bible (KJV). The Holy Bible, New International Version (NIV). Copyright © 1973, 1978, 1984 International Bible Society. Used by permission of Zondervan Bible Publishers. The Revised Standard Version of the Bible (RSV), copyrighted 1946, 1952, © 1971, 1973 by the Division of Christian Education of the National Council of the Churches of Christ in the U.S.A., and are used by permission.

Library of Congress Cataloging-in-Publication Data

Anderson, Deacon, 1928–
    The way back : a Christian's journey to mental wholeness / Deacon
    Anderson, Robert C. Richard.
        p.   cm.
    ISBN 0-8499-0730-6
    1. Anderson, Deacon, 1928–   . 2. Christian biography—United
States. 3. Psychotherapy—Religious aspects—Christianity.
I. Richard, Robert C., 1938–   . II. Title.
BR1725.A6684A34   1989
261.5'15—dc20   89-12422
                                                                        CIP

Printed in the United States of America

9 8 0 1 2 3 9   BKC   9 8 7 6 5 4 3 2 1

To
Mary, my wife and best friend,
and to
Mark, Barbara, and Scott,
who shared part of the journey

—Deacon

To
my wife, Shirley,
and
sons, David and John—
the support of those closest means the most.

—Robert

Contents

How This Book Came to Be Written

It was a late afternoon in the spring. Deacon Anderson sat across from me in my office. It had been over a year since he first came to see me, a desperate and emotionally dying man seeking help. He was a different man now, and we shared a deep sense of accomplishment and satisfaction over the profound changes that had occurred in his life.

The psychotherapy sojourn had often been difficult and demanding, but the exhilaration and excitement of seeing Deacon's life take on a new dimension of aliveness and fulfillment had made it all worthwhile. How wonderful it had been to see him move from death to life, from a darkness that possessed his spirit to a light that began to permeate the most remote corners of his soul.

As we talked that day of Deacon's progress, we also reflected on the pervasive sense of God's presence that had been evident throughout the process. Because we are both Christians and share some basic perspectives about God's work in the world and the human being's place in the universe, we understood that God was at work in the psychotherapeutic process. Not only was he at work there, but he also used that very process to make himself more fully known.

As Deacon and I talked, an idea was born, tentatively at first, but then with increasing clarity. Why not share this process of change, not simply as a "case study" but as a deeply human/spiritual experience told from two perspectives—that of the client *and* that of the psychotherapist?

Such an account would allow other persons to see "inside" the process through the eyes of *both* recipient and facilitator. Perhaps approaching the psychotherapy process in this manner could further "demystify" it for others and reinforce it as an important option leading to the healing of mental and emotional disorders.

Our idea took concrete form in the book you now hold in your hands. The format is unique for a book on this subject. Deacon first expresses his experience which I then follow in each case with comments that are designed to help the reader better understand Deacon's struggle and ultimate healing, as well as to shed some light on why I selected certain therapeutic interventions to bring about needed change.

In this account we take the term *psychotherapy* to mean "the treatment of disability in the mind." In contrast to counseling, which is primarily aimed at problem solving, psychotherapy works at curing mental disability through changes in one's perceptions, thinking patterns, emotions, and behavior. These are changes which are noticed by others as well as the person participating in the therapy. A more positive attitude toward other persons and one's self, new ways of coping with stress, resolution of old hurts, a new sense of meaning and direction in life—all may become apparent.

Due to the historic tension between psychology and Christian theology, many, if not most, Christians view psychology and psychotherapy with a wary eye. To the extent that psychotherapy has mistakenly denied the importance and validity of personal religious experience, wariness on the part of Christians is understandable. Fortunately, however, we do not have to make a choice between faith and psychotherapy. The latter need not destroy the former. Indeed, it is a *central point* of our account that a psychotherapist who views a client's faith as an integral part of his or her life experience also sees it as a potentially powerful force in the creation of new patterns of thinking, feeling, and behaving. Faith and psychotherapy do not have to be at war. To the contrary, each stands ready to assist the other and inform the other; and both share the common goal of helping the person become all he or she was meant to be in the eyes of God.

The journey of personal growth has never been an easy one in any century. Today psychotherapy opens up another avenue, a latter-day path which allows us to partake of the presence of God as he seeks to bring healing to disabled minds. If psychotherapy and faith have been enemies, it is only our perceptions that have made them so.

ROBERT C. RICHARD, PH.D.
Pleasant Hill, California

Introduction

The woods are lovely, dark and deep.
But I have promises to keep,
And miles to go before I sleep,
And miles to go before I sleep.

—Robert Frost*

Not for a moment in the pre-therapy months did I think there was anything that would or could change the decline in my fortunes. I was like a boxer hauling myself off the stool and facing my opponent for what would probably be the last round. I had not acquitted myself well. I was bone tired. I had taken severe punishment, and I hurt everywhere. I was absolutely stuck with my lot in life. No one could save me. No one could give me relief. I could not win, and as long as there was life in me, I could not quit. To quit would be to dishonor myself. I would have to absorb whatever came my way until the fight had run its inevitable course.

That is exactly the way I felt about the situation I found myself in. And I had not felt that way for just a few days. I had felt that way for fifty years! My condition was hopeless. I was *right about that*—at least for the first several years of my life when I was dependent upon and wholly subject to the control of others. But when I turned to therapy as the next-to-the-last resort (the last resort would be to quit life), I learned

* Copyright 1923 by Holt, Rinehart and Winston, Inc., and renewed 1951 by Robert Frost. Reprinted from *The Poetry of Robert Frost*, edited by Edward Connery Lathem, by permission of Henry Holt and Company, Inc.

that in all those years I had been *wrong about myself*. I had associated the circumstances of my childhood environment with who I was as a person, and I had paid the price of absorbing galling punishment and of waiting . . . waiting . . . interminable waiting for I knew not what.

As a Christian, I knew I was not alone in my misery. God was with me, but the pain was no less excruciating. In fact, I found it hurt all the more because the absence of change *appeared* to be God's expression of approval for the condition. What other way of thinking could I have? After all, the *sovereign* God could have done *something* about it if he really wanted to. Couldn't he?

I prayed. Oh, how I prayed. I surrendered—a thousand times, I surrendered. I "claimed" victory, only to have defeat laugh in my face. I pleaded, I begged, I cajoled, I bargained, I confessed, I worked with pleasure within the church, I praised . . . and I worsened. I worked without pleasure, to the same effect. I quit trying to do anything about my situation, allowing God to do whatever he would do . . . and I worsened. I cried out, "Who will deliver me from this body of death?" and I responded, "Thanks be to God through Jesus Christ our Lord!" . . . and I worsened.

As you can see, this book is about mental anguish. But it is much more than that. It is also a book about *promise fulfilled*. The pain is memory now, replaced by a heaping measure of joy and contentment. Through therapy I made peace with my beginnings, and now each day I look forward to life.

My Christian faith has grown through this process in a way it could not have grown before—*growth made possible by the absence of defense mechanisms which were rendered unnecessary by the therapy process*. There is, however, a problem in writing about my experience. It may seem to belie the sincerity of my early Christian faith. And some may feel that I mean I have lost my faith. I have not. My faith was on solid ground before therapy and remains on solid ground today. I have grown as a person, and my faith has kept pace.

Robert Richard and I have written this book to let others know that there is hope for those who struggle with mental anguish. Help *is* available. This very account might be for you or a loved one the first step of heaven-sent intervention. The book will not make you well, but it may give you suggestions for how wellness—that wonderful feeling of mental fitness and joy of life—might be yours.

How to Read This Book

As you read the first two chapters, keep in mind that I have written this account in the present tense to re-create as faithfully as possible my feelings prior to and in the early phases of therapy. (In other words, these chapters do not reflect my present mind-set.) Restricting that writing to the present tense also made it impossible to fudge, to peek ahead to the time when therapy began to explain why I felt that way. This also allows you, the reader, to walk with me as I walked from desperation and confusion to mental wholeness.

Much of the book was written in the heat of discovery, using material taken from a journal I started when I began therapy. I made journal entries with no intention of writing a book. The entries used here are verbatim with additions for clarification set in brackets. Journal entries are treated as excerpts and are set off from the rest of the text.

Deacon Anderson
Moraga, California

The WAY BACK

I.

THE VALLEY

A time when life narrows and hope wanes and God seems impotent

Let me alone, that I may take comfort a little, Before I go whence I shall not return, even to the land of darkness and the shadow of death.

—Job 10:20–21, KJV

ANDERSON:

At fifty-six, I am in moderately good health—if you will allow a significant discount on the spare tire I have carried around for twenty years—and yet my life is over.

I have a great wife, a good family of mostly grown children, a fine job with an excellent company. I have enough money to cover all the necessities of life and most of the wants. I have adequate social status and a usually satisfying spiritual life. I labored successfully in television news for many years. My life has been given over to Jesus Christ. I have nothing that is not going for me.

And I am bored to death—or to dying, anyway—dying on my feet without ever having lived.

There is a stretch of highway I–5 in the Tehachapi Mountains north of Los Angeles where the road descends steadily towards Bakersfield. Until the braking system on trucks

1

improved a few years ago, truckers were advised to check their brakes at the top of the treacherous "grapevine," as the road is commonly referred to, before starting downhill. Not infrequently truckers had the terrifying and sometimes deadly experience of having the brakes fail on the miles-long slope. If the brakes burned out, the truckers' *only* hope was to steer into one of the deep sand traps that had been placed at intervals along the road. If they managed to do this, they might get out alive.

I'm on my own "grapevine" right now. I must have missed the warning signs at the top of the grade. At least I didn't stop and check the brakes, and now I find this truck I call "me" picking up speed. It started so gradually. I was ticking right along, passing up a lot of others and things looked great, but now I'm aware that I'm going too fast. I find now that I'm using every ounce of energy and skill I have to keep this life on the road. The brakes are burned out, and I can't get the rig slowed down enough to get into a lower gear. If I try to shift down now, it will tear out the gear box.

I don't have total control of myself, and I'm not on a road of my own choosing. The crazy thing about it is that while I know I'm not going to get out of this mess, I still function quite well. Now that I know I'm doomed, I do what I can not to hurt others before my ride comes to its end. I can't seem to make it over to one of the sand traps. You would think this process of dying would be exciting, but it's not. It is insufferably boring.

It is a fact that my life has not turned out at all as I had hoped it would. I never was a starry-eyed dreamer, but I had really expected something better, if not far better, than what has come my way in this experience called life.

The earnest and hopeful expectations of my earliest years were not based on qualities I felt I possessed. I have been forever uncertain that I actually possess any good qualities I can call mine. And being born in the parsonage of an honest evangelical minister, my hopes were certainly not built on the expectation of inherited fortunes.

I have always been too much a realist to think I *deserved* better than I have received. Quite the opposite. I'm unable to specify skills or talents that justify what I have received. Maybe it was God, in his grace, giving from his bounty to the undeserving. Maybe it was just dumb luck. Whatever it was, I have done all right in the matter of earning money and receiving some modicum of acclaim. *But yet, for most of my life I expected better than I got.*

My earlier optimism, such as it was, was not based just on wishful thinking. It was based on observing how people mature. People are like butterflies growing out of the cocoon of their youth to become fully functioning adults. Some people turn out to be fantastically beautiful; others are not so beautiful but still they are butterflies. It seems to be some developmental law of nature that some day things sort themselves out for young people and thereafter they take upon themselves a new and handsome identity.

It didn't happen that way with me. I have spent my life metamorphosing all right, but from butterfly to cocoon. Not that I considered myself beautiful to begin with. I have never felt that about myself. But I did consider that *some* potential for happiness and competence had once been there. It is the feeling of *loss of the potential to be a beautiful butterfly* that has manifested itself by folding my unformed wings, tucking in my head and my tail, curling up my arms and legs, and letting the circumstances of my life bind me in a blanket of isolation and tuck me away somewhere; unseeing, unhearing, unseen, and unsaying. I am deep into the cocoon stage of this inverted metamorphosis. If I survive, it shall be as a stiff and ugly caterpillar, inching my way across the fast track, hoping not to get run over in the process.

There has been no turning point, no milepost of which I can say, "*That* was when my world began to fall apart." It would be so emotionally satisfying to point to *something*—say, the death of my father—and say "There it is. That is what did me in." No, I have thought this through about as thoroughly as I can, and there has been no pivotal great moment when my life began to go downhill. The slope has been slight, which has made my regress all the more maddening. I can find nothing to blame . . . but myself.

However, flipping back the pages of my life, I realize that vocationally at least, it started well. After a stint as a newspaper reporter and wire-service editor, I made a leap into television news. In less than a year, I moved from Omaha to San Francisco, and there I was one of the very small army of people who invented and nurtured the television newscast.

It was an exciting time. The several of us in the early days of television journalism had a secret. We knew the medium was going to have at least as great an impact on news coverage as Gutenberg's movable type had had on the dissemination of Scripture. We were aware we were blazing a trail through virgin territory. We were going where no one had ever gone. Technology was on our side, allowing us to grow from film to tape, from black and white to color, from heavy cameras to light cameras, to live transmissions from remote sites, to use of television satellites. In a dedicated and creative style, we rode the crest of changing technology and public fascination. Very important people recognized what was happening and called us by our first names.

An exhilarating ride it was.

We earned our spurs every night at six o'clock, and we deserved all the credit we received. It was a dizzy, crazy ride, and the demands it made upon me, my contribution to its development, my professional success, and the accompanying public recognition which I longed for and received, gave monumental recompense for the virtually comatose person who cried, unheard, within me.

In unexpected moments of quietude, I shuddered at the recurring notion that I might be constructing a house of cards which would one day come crashing down around me. I dreaded the day when those in power would discover that anyone could do what I was doing and would throw me out on the street. If by invested energy or just plain chance I fooled them again today, I would get another opportunity tomorrow. Television was easy. It was *life* that was hard to figure out.

DR. RICHARD:

Before Deacon Anderson crossed the threshold of my office, he was engaged in a consuming psychological struggle. The struggle was not new; it had been part of his existence in one form or another for many years. But now the struggle had become acute.

For many persons the antecedents of psychological struggles are evident, sometimes obvious. But for others there is nothing obvious. In fact, outwardly there may be numerous appearances of success. For these persons the sources of psychological disturbance lie in early experiences, many of which remain outside of conscious recollections. But the impact of these early experiences remains alive, supporting patterns of thinking, feeling, and behaving that often impede such persons from finding a happy and fulfilling existence.

It was all the more confusing to Deacon, because while at one level he had a definite sense that something was missing and that he deserved more, at another level he felt he was *not* deserving. This doubt about deserving something better went to the core of his being. He began to think that what he had gotten or achieved was only by the grace of God or just "dumb luck." What Deacon confronted here is one form of a self-esteem struggle. There was a strong sense of potential somehow missed and yet a parallel sense that the actualization of such potential was not deserved. This is a mind game that utterly blocks the possibility for personal change and growth with a consequent continuation of a deadly, stultifying *status quo*. Rooted deep in his past, this self-esteem struggle helped shape Deacon's life in ways which escaped his consciousness. He experienced the results of the struggle but did not understand just how it was affecting him and from whence it came.

Our perceptions of ourselves—that is, how we feel about ourselves and think about ourselves—have enormous and encompassing implications for the way we live our lives. Self-perceptions are formed early in life and are derived from various sources, but they are especially connected with parental messages and other significant experiences with important family members or other authority figures. Carried into adult life, self-perceptions may hold the seeds of blessing or the seeds of curse. For most people it is usually a mixture of the two. For Deacon, the seeds of curse predominated.

As it is with many persons, especially males, Deacon looked to his vocational successes as a way of assuring himself that all was well. In the midst of his "exhilarating ride," there were the quiet times when deep, interior doubts forced themselves to the surface. And Deacon would reason, "if a man does well in his chosen work, then *he must be all right.*" But pain comes when the success in work does not really heal the self-doubts. Deacon could not experience healing through his work because, as beneficial as vocational success was, it did not reach to the level in Deacon's being where healing was needed. So much confusion exists here, both for Deacon and others: For psychological healing and integration to occur, intervention must be made at the level appropriate to the *source* of the problem experienced. Mistaken intervention leads to little or no change.

For instance, many people look to change their exterior circumstances as a way of dealing with essentially internal conflicts. Thus a marriage is ended and a new one begun, a job is terminated and a new one sought, the old community is left and a new community is found. However, internal conflicts are often not resolved by such changes, and the individual is dismayed to find himself or herself dealing with some of the very same problems which were being dealt with prior to the external change.

ANDERSON:

In my television news days, the excesses of my life could have been seen as signals that all was not right. But I was then at the top of the grapevine looking down that marvelous highway instead of at any warning signs.

I smoked too much. That should have told me something. In today's environment, we have a fuller understanding that any smoking is too much. I was on three packs a day plus cigars and pipes. I lit a cigarette before I got up in the morning and put the last one out after I turned off the light at night. When I quit smoking for the last time, it was a matter of choosing between smoking and breathing, so I quit smoking. Quitting did nothing for my head problems, but it did give my lungs a treat.

Looking back, another sign I missed was drinking. I didn't drink regularly, nor even frequently, but when I did drink, I drank a lot. Some drink too much and get belligerent. Not me. Too much alcohol made me sentimental in an unfocused way. I got the peculiar inner sensation of almost remembering something which was probably very good or very happy. Layered beneath that was the suspicion that if I could remember what that "something" was, I would be very sad. I didn't know why.

DR. RICHARD:

Mind-altering drugs, legal and illegal, are taken for a variety of purposes. *But drugs become a serious problem when they are integrated into one's life as an integral way of coping with internal conflicts and external demands.* Drugs affect symptoms only and never deal with underlying causes of a problem except in disorders where the source of the difficulty may be traced to brain biochemistry. In reality the use of drugs may severely cloud one's ability to get to the true source of psychological pain or discomfort. While symptom reduction via drugs may provide some relief, it may also produce a false assurance of well-being. Certainly the nicotine and alcohol Deacon used did nothing toward the healing he needed to experience.

The seduction of drugs lies in their quick mood alteration. But the price to be paid over time is failure to achieve healing at the level which generates the symptoms. Deacon's experience with these common drugs was really no different from that of many others. Fortunately, however, Deacon's struggle toward wholeness did not terminate, as so often happens, in a quagmire of chemicals.

ANDERSON:

As a television news director, I thought of myself as being as necessary to the newsroom as electricity was to the camera. Only the news director knew everything that was going on. I never felt I was off work—not at nights, not on weekends, not even on vacations. There may have been some modicum of truth to this perception, but only a modicum.

I worked then for the same reason I work now—because I'm scared. Or maybe I work in spite of the fact I'm scared. Call it wall-to-wall anxiety, nonstop angst. Call it what you will, there is an arcane foreboding always flitting through my mind. In my early days it was an invisible cloud of pending doom which only I knew about. It still is. I could perform well, eleven hours a day, seven days a week, giving instructions, making assignments, working out production decisions, coaching the broadcasters—I still can—but I couldn't shake that feeling that something awful was going to happen. I still can't.

I was then, and continue to be, a professional "anxietist." As a writer must write to be a writer, an anxietist must constantly feed the mind with reasons for his uneasiness. I legitimize my worry by seeing as a threat to my career almost any unexpected thing which happens. And that which threatens my career threatens my livelihood, and thus my very life. I left television news after twenty years to manage the television department of a very large corporation. Many things changed but not my anxiety habits. I carried those bags with me when I changed vocational trains.

My response to anxiety is eating. I eat frequently and bountifully. I take more pleasure in eating than in almost anything else, and my waistline is witness to my gastronomical sins. My mother trained me to eat as a safe response to stress, and I was a good student. It takes but a glance to see how much stress I have been under lately, and how faithfully I have adhered to my childhood lessons. While I am not entirely indiscriminate in my eating habits, neither am I a gourmet. Eating is my pacifier, mother, nurse, and psychiatrist. I enjoy it and never pass up the opportunity to attend to it.

As the years toll on, anxiety has taken the form of worry that I will soon be fired, although I haven't done anything worth getting fired for. Maybe "they" will decide I haven't done much of anything and fire me for that. Or, maybe I will be forcibly retired, or transferred. Professional successes notwithstanding, "they" will find out I really didn't have any skills. I will have to throw myself on their mercy, whomever "they" might be. Will they listen?

Such thinking processes orbit tirelessly through my brain, but that is the only thing that is tireless. I am chronically bone tired. I generally feel like I've been on a thirty-mile forced march under the authority of the least kindly of first sergeants.

There have been very few moments when I wasn't tired to the depths of my being. I was an exhausted three-year-old, for heaven's sake! Fortunately, I was born with an ability to work well—acceptably anyway—no matter how exhausted I become. It doesn't seem to deplete my business judgments.

DR. RICHARD:

Deacon was haunted by the demon of anxiety. Anxiety pervaded his life. It came as a foreboding, an unrelenting sense of threat, an irrational worry. Associated with this anxiety were all manner of fearful fantasies, especially surrounding his work. Vocational success was a bastion he had erected against the powerful waves of self-doubt. Should that bastion fail, the profound inner sense of worthlessness would indeed be overwhelming. "What if" thinking, which led to imagined disastrous outcomes, increasingly occupied Deacon's thoughts. Associated with all of this fearful thinking was his experience of energy depletion. It takes energy to cope with excessive levels of anxiety. Energy that could be used in creative and constructive ways, instead, is focused on fearful thinking, resulting in tense muscles (which also use up precious energy) or other physiological symptoms.

Deacon's response to his anxiety was eating, a practice that he recognized was learned early on from his mother. From childhood days, Deacon had found eating worked consistently well in anxiety reduction, even though in later life the trade-off was a constantly enlarging abdomen. To him this was a price worth paying. The comforting association he made with mother, eating, and feeling safe and secure by now had become well established. Many persons recognize that overeating is a response to their anxiety, while others recognize that cessation of appetite may be their response to anxiety. All of this points to the fact that many, though not all, eating problems have psychological roots. This fact is being increasingly recognized by the more sophisticated weight-reduction programs which combine diet with psychological insights.

When pervasive anxiety (in contrast to transient or situational anxiety) infects our lives, it is all too easy to get focused on *how* we feel and *what* to do to reduce our intense feelings of uneasiness. Most people do not realize it, but anxiety carries a message about ourselves and our lives. To simply reduce the symptoms of anxiety and not try to understand what is causing the anxiety is like trying to fix a piece of dry-rotted wood with a coat of paint. It may look and feel acceptable on the outside, but it is crumbling on the inside. And rot will continue unless the underlying process which produces the condition is corrected.

Failure to understand and come to terms with the roots of pervasive anxiety will only lead to ongoing struggle, with battles won and lost, but the war never ended. Thus, anxiety carries within it the seeds of great personal growth, for its driving uncomfortableness may ultimately force us to deal with painful issues which we might otherwise work desperately hard to avoid, and in so doing miss the pathway to significant personal fulfillment.

ANDERSON:

As I mentioned earlier, I have a suspicion that I've been missing something all these years, something that is perfectly obvious but that I just can't see. It's like searching for your keys or your glasses only to find them right where they belong. They've been there all the time, but for whatever reasons you didn't see the obvious.

So it is with this feeling that I have endured some great and wholly unnecessary loss over all these years. It's almost there, like an old and familiar name which I know but just can't quite dredge up right now. It is not that I don't want to find that missing element. I have tried, oh, how I have tried. I have even tried to sneak up on myself to see if I would blurt out whatever it is that is just beyond my mental reach. It's like having an itch that you can't scratch.

One of the ways I try to scratch that itch, especially after a particularly bad or boring day, is to daydream that I am being interviewed by a friendly, almost adoring television talk-show host. On the show I am a very successful writer— or musician, sculptor, comedian, philosopher, or theologian —eminent in my field. I'm not on the show to promote a book or anything like that. I'm there because the host really wants me and I really want to share of my life.

The host asks me how I came by my success, and I am pleased to give good and honest answers which, contrary to my intent, never quite give the exact reason for my success. With each answer, I seem to be closer than I was on the last question. I'm now only a shade away from the *root* answer. The host poses *the* question. I smile and give *the* answer— only to realize that it isn't quite *the* answer after all. There is something still deeper and more profound yet to be revealed . . . and the host asks the next question.

The daydream ends when the host runs out of questions and I run out of answers. The daydream begins as a satisfying experience, but it ends up as very unsatisfying and disconcerting because I have not divulged nor learned the secret of my success.

Daydreaming is a haunting distraction because it is evidence that there is something hidden very deep inside me. From my daydreams, I conclude that I really *could* have been some of those things had my life circumstance been different—had I not been born in a parsonage, had I married someone else, continued further in school, taken a job with CBS, or not resigned the high-status job I held for several years. The premise of the recurrent daydream is that I am trying to account for imagined success. Lurking backstage is the truth: I am searching for the reason for my lifelong *sense of failure*. And I can't even succeed in searching out the reason for my sense of failure.

DR. RICHARD:

Very often an ongoing sense of "something missing" comes to consciousness during the midlife transition. It is during this period of adult development that most persons engage in sporadic or systematic reflection on their lives. This, combined with the dawning awareness that life on this earth really does have an end, that time on this planet really will run out, often produces an intense search for "what is missing." The search may involve various significant lifestyle changes such as new vocational directions, divorce and remarriage, geographical change, and resetting of values and priorities. *Such changes may or may not be helpful, depending on their true relationship to "what is missing."* Many are the persons who have made rather drastic changes in their lives only to find that the changes put them no closer to "what is missing" than they were before.

For Deacon daydreaming became a way of trying to get at what he lacked. In the daydream Deacon was vocationally successful, and the television talk-show host wanted him there for reasons beyond his success: that is, he was *wanted for himself*. This was a major clue to what was missing for Deacon, but he did not recognize it yet. However, what Deacon did recognize, and this is *extremely important*, is that there was indeed something hidden deep *inside* of him. It was not "out there" but within, and the route to discovery would require an inward journey. Also coming out of the fantasy is another important realization: Back of the imagined sense of success was the lurking, black shadow of a permeating sense of failure. This was another way of experiencing and expressing the feeling of not being a deserving person; it was another manifestation of the self-esteem struggle.

Daydreaming can be a wonderful pastime. It can carry us to places where we have never been, to people we would like to encounter, to accomplishments we have never known. In fact, out of daydreams have come some of the great, creative ideas that have helped shape our world. Marvelous accomplishments always start as a human fantasy. Because daydreams are necessarily a product of the daydreamer, they often yield important information about that person. Recurrent daydreams are especially important, for they play on themes that point, sometimes clearly, sometimes obtusely, toward inward pain and distress. Daydreams can become vital internal communicators helping us to assess our state of being. However, daydreams may also become an end in themselves. They may in fact be used as an escape from self-awareness in order to bring solace and comfort. Used in this manner, they may be considered a "mental drug" used to reduce symptoms, but their value as major clues to inward longings or conflicts becomes lost.

ANDERSON:

Before I talk about my married life, you should know that I have always loved my wife, even when I hated her. Before we were married, Mary's qualities were very clear to me. She was fun. She was extraordinarily beautiful. She was smart. She had more pep and energy than any two people I have ever met. And she was fearless.

However, I have come to feel that Mary doesn't love me and never did. Perhaps it is my scrambled thinking process, perhaps not, but I detect no feeling for me at all, not even a fondness. I am there and that is that. When I used to say, "I love you," she would sometimes reflect my sentiments back, sometimes not. It may be that only ranch women who wear rhinestones and live on celluloid say "I love you" to the chief wrangler. I don't remember Mary's ever initiating such sentiments toward me.

On one thing we will have no disagreement: Love is a tough cookie, but it is also fragile. If you have to ask someone if they love you because you're not sure they do, then no matter how warmly they respond, it is not a spontaneous expression. It's like teasing "Polly want a cracker" out of a parrot.

On the other hand, if you have to ask someone if they love you, is it really love you feel for the other person? Love is not something that must be reciprocated. Love for someone is without the expectation of any kind of reward, including love returned.

If in my way of thinking Mary didn't love me, why in my way of thinking did she marry me? I came up with a lot of reasons for that.

I decided that, even though she didn't find me very interesting in the way of intimate sharing, she enjoyed what I could provide: a good income, some recognition by my peers in a glamour industry, recognition by her peers and the public, a chance to be a first-nighter at many of the best social and entertainment affairs in San Francisco. Mary brought to the marriage her great beauty, her smarts, tremendous homemaker talents, a frisky personality which inevitably made her well liked, and a work ethic that went to the core of her being. Put it together as we did, and you have a tolerable marriage. That was it—tolerable. She could have married much better. Early on, I came to know she had to live with her one big mistake in life—me. She has never said anything like that, but I know.

When we began having children, Mary proved to be a four star mother. She lavished love and patience on our three children, and the bonding between mother and child was, and remains, astonishing. My love for them matches Mary's, but I have never quite made it with the bonding. They are grown now, and I love them and their spouses with a depth that words could never encompass. But they remain their mother's children. That is to be expected, I guess. There was no bonding whatever between my father and me. But *I hate missing the closeness I think should exist between my children and me*, too.

It brings me no comfort to know that the fulsome dissatisfaction with myself is what is creating a dreadful breach between myself and my wife and children. That I don't want to contaminate them with my morbidity is not a noble thought. I cannot even take credit for my isolation. It has simply come upon me in the course of this experience, but I celebrate with mirthless joy that the normal course I follow tends to distance me from those I hold most dear so they won't pick up the disease. This cancer of the spirit, which is taking its sustenance from my mental vitals, is so powerful I can't help but think it is likely to be highly contagious.

Sometimes I think I see in those I love traces of the thousand things I hate about me. Are these traces some genetic hand-me-down I have passed on? Will they carry through the next generation? To see a loathsome trait in them is horrifying and disgusting. I want to excise it and leave them whole, but of course I can't. Yet at times I scold the person for the action or attitude I dislike. It is accurate to say I hate to see anything I dislike about myself reflected in my children or my wife.

DR. RICHARD:

A personal psychological struggle always affects our relationships with those around us. Nowhere is this felt more keenly than in relationships which have the greatest meaning. For most people those relationships are with one's spouse, children, parents, and close friends. In Deacon's case, he raised questions about the quality of love in his

marriage. He doubted that his wife loved him, or more accurately, he did not feel she loved him at all. In struggling
to cope with this unpleasant experience, he believed that he
indeed was the source of the problem. He concluded that
his wife had married him for reasons other than a deep love
and caring for him. Deacon now saw himself as simply an
instrument for meeting his wife's social, material, and
recognition needs.

As we shall see later, Deacon was unconsciously caught in
a psychological web spun from the material of his past. The
truth is that what human beings expect from a loving relationship is inextricably intertwined with what they have or
have not received from previous encounters, especially in
their parental families. These early experiences are so powerful that they play a significant role regarding whom we
choose to marry. Paradoxically, these early learnings about
love may compel us to move toward persons who will indeed help provide a quality of loving we lacked. On the
other hand, these very learnings may keep us from what we
need. We have become "comfortable" with our love patterns; they form part of the total picture of who we are, and
they shape the way we "fit" into loving relationships. Thus,
the woman who experiences distorted loving at the hands of
an emotionally abusive father *may* choose, unconsciously, a
husband who continues the pattern of abuse which "fits"
the woman so well. Or take, for example, the man with a
passive and emotionally dry mother who may end up with
a wife who also has difficulty expressing feelings and engaging in closeness. Or the woman who, though chafing under
her father's overbearing control, nevertheless marries a
strong male who continues to direct her life. Examples, in
their multifaceted variations, go on and on. Of course, there
are those who more or less consciously choose love relationships which will give them an experience much different
from what they have had before. In so doing, they take the
risk that the "fit" will not be as comfortable. In making a

new fit, the man or woman may struggle with loving or being loved in new or different ways to which they have not been accustomed. These new ways may even feel somewhat "alien" to them. Thus they may feel that they do not deserve the love they are receiving, or that the loving is too demanding, or that closeness is too threatening.

However, the central point here is that when we feel we are not getting the kind of loving we want with our spouses, the answers lie not so much in blaming the failings on our husband or wife, but in how *we* have participated in the creation of a scenario that keeps us from getting what we want or need. True, Deacon blamed himself, but not in a healthy, insightful way. At this point he was not aware of how his own experiences of loving and how he felt about himself contributed to his choice of a mate and to his perception of how his wife loved him. The key to his understanding of what he was needing and could get really lay inside himself.

There was also in Deacon a concern that he somehow had not been the kind of father to his children that he could have been. He sensed that his emotional struggle had crippled him from relating to his children in ways that would have been more beneficial to them.

It is probably fair to say that virtually all parents, reflecting on their parenting skills, become conscious of failings that give rise to feelings of remorse, self-blame, and guilt. As with our spouses, the quality of love we experienced as children goes a long way toward influencing how we feel and behave in the loving relationships we have with our children. Since, as we shall see, Deacon's experiences of love with his parents were badly flawed, he was not certain just what emotionally healthy loving toward his own children should be. He certainly had some rational ideas about what it should be, but he had very little to go on at a deeply felt emotional level.

If we listen to ourselves closely, we may become quite aware that at times we are hearing our own parents speaking through us to *our* children. What is even more disconcerting is when we see ourselves speaking and acting in ways that our parents did toward us but that we vowed we would *never* do with our own children. Such an experience is not an isolated event, but somewhat common and is simply testimony to the powerful early learning of childhood.

The tendency toward replicating with our children what we experienced at the hands of our parents is strong. Obviously those parts of our upbringing which were emotionally healthy deserve repeating. But those parts which were destructive need to be exorcised from our child-raising endeavors and replaced with approaches which demonstrate quality loving.

Those who have had poor parental models, as did Deacon, often feel they are "out on their own" trying to create anew ways of relating to their children which they strongly sense and believe are emotionally healthy; but, because they have no emotional bank of experience on which to draw, they lack certitude about being on the mark.

Deacon wondered if somehow his problems would be passed on to his children. This nightmarish thought caused him to recoil upon viewing any negative aspect of himself manifested in his offspring or even his wife. To see parts of ourselves that we do not like appearing in our children is really inevitable since they are both genetically and behaviorally our direct descendants.

In some cases generations of descendants are emotionally and mentally crippled by the repeated emergence in the family of destructive patterns of relating. Thus we observe successive generations affected by child abuse, alcoholism or other drug addition, spouse abuse, violence, and generally unstable and volatile relationships. The biblical statement that the iniquities of the fathers are visited upon the children of the third and fourth generation (Exodus 20:5) may, psychologically, be considered literally true.

These patterns may go on unabated unless there is some

intervention which will powerfully alter the destructive ways of relating to other family members as well as to one's self. Such intervention may come from different sources, but it *must* come. As yet unknown to Deacon was the fact that he would enter into an intervention process that would powerfully change how he felt and thought about himself and others, a change which was profoundly needed but which was beyond his grasp at this point in his journey to mental wholeness.

ANDERSON:

I am in mortal combat. A soldier can be ordered to go into combat and be told how to behave in that predicament and be told not to be scared, but he can't be ordered not to be scared. It is not the option of an outside agency to determine if another will be afraid of something. That will happen within the subject without regard to outside resources. It's like telling a man he's not going to die. Unless the guy who is speaking is God, it is a vacuous assurance.

I am an expert on how to behave, when to shoot, when to rest, when to crawl forward, and I respond fairly much according to accepted standards. But I am afraid—afraid of everything. If one could be assessed by his expenditure of energy rather than by his accomplishments, I would go down as a heroic figure of contemporary life because by sheer guts I dutifully meet the demands placed upon me in the home, at church, and in the marketplace. My energy is expended fighting down the terrors within; and I am losing. But I am fighting, and I will continue to fight.

Yet I am alarmed that my ability to concentrate is dissipating. What has happened to the single-mindedness that made an enjoyable challenge of monitoring a hundred things going on in a noisy, crowded, smoky newsroom? My mind no longer tracks anything but the deepening shadow of my sadness. Thoughts are waterbugs skittering about, pausing here and there, sampling a thousand things but stopping for nothing. I can't read for very long, nor watch much television, nor even carry on a long conversation. Any mental activity makes me restless. *I'm trapped and must escape.*

A poor memory for isolated facts has always been a handicap, but now it's become a serious problem, bothersome in the extreme. There is an irony in what I can and can't remember. The things I can remember are the bad things about me. I am unable to remember anything good about me. Surely there must have been *something* good about me.

DR. RICHARD:

As Deacon passed through the middle stage of his life, he was confronted by an acute dread born of a sense of personal emptiness and despair. The terrible dread, however, was affecting his ability to concentrate and thus to remember well. Lack of concentration, which directly affects our ability to remember, is a hallmark of high anxiety levels. It is a message about the state of our being. While temporary lapses in concentration may be directly related to a given situation, such as a boring conversation, an irrelevant class in school, a meaningless job, and so forth, an ongoing concentration problem surfacing over a wide variety of situations indicates a pervasive problem.

Furthermore, Deacon was becoming aware that what he did remember was usually negative things about himself. He had become caught in the net of "selective negative thinking," systematically excluding self-affirming remembrances and focusing instead on the downgrading and critical.

Persons with significant self-esteem problems nearly always become caught in this selective-negative-thinking net. Unfortunately this net has the effect of reinforcing poor self-esteem by locking the individual into a circular perceptual process which runs something like this: Since this person does not think of himself as a good person, he does not really wish to see or remember those things which positively affirm him or make him feel good. Such things really do not fit well with how he views himself. But those things which *do* fit well are those which affirm what he perceives as his inadequacy, worthlessness, and badness. Those are the things he can more easily perceive and remember. This process is generally unconscious, but it is insidious. And for the person with damaged self-esteem, the process may likely remain remarkably stable unless there is intervention at a level which will break the cycle of selective negative thinking.

ANDERSON:

Another problem is my impatience with people. Almost anything—a slow response in conversation, a clarifying question, the misreading of a note, a phone call that isn't answered within three rings—will trigger enough anger to make me turn away or hang up in disgust. Almost everything done by, to, or for me becomes a candidate for my criticism.

It takes no genius to know that my reaction to people who are just being themselves is a turn-off to them. I just don't care anymore. I am too tired to care. The result of my emotional fatigue is that I am having less and less contact with others; not just with casual or business friends, but also with my closer church friends and my family, including my wife. My withdrawal pattern has, over time, developed a life cycle of its own—a downward spiral of silent criticism of others and withdrawal from them.

As I find myself being alone for long periods, I wonder if one day I will cease to communicate directly with anyone. Observe them, yes, but communicate with them? Well, not if I can help it.

With my social life in ruins, it is understandable that my effectiveness at work is on the decline. At times those who report to me seem to be unwitting participants in a conspiracy to diminish what little effectiveness remains. Once they were able and interested in pleasing me. But, no more. I know this is not a plot, but it might as well be. I take this "unconspiracy" as additional reason to avoid contact with those who report to me, and with those to whom I report. Thus I am isolating myself from normal contact with all my work associates. If at all possible, I avoid seeing or talking to others. I communicate when I must by using memos.

I question my judgments, all of them. I can hardly make a decision. These are not complex decisions to make. My subordinates and my boss make these same kinds of decisions all the time. I know others see me as I see myself—weak and not qualified to address issues of any importance. I get by, if that's the right expression, by forcing others—Mary, co-workers, friends—to make all decisions. They do it so easily, these important others. The people at work allude to my indecisiveness now and then—"Well, make your decision and then let me know"—and that in and of itself is proof that I don't even have the sense to make reasonable judgments. They are so competent and able, and I am neither competent nor able. Anyone can see that. My self-confidence has bottomed out.

And there's the new boss who measures life in terms of clout, position, and money. He is the final straw that broke my spirit.

I am at the point where I get *no* satisfaction out of work. *None. Zero. Zip.* I work only in order to bring home the money the family needs to live.

I no longer control my destiny.

DR. RICHARD:

Exactly how our social and work relationships are influenced by our personal struggles depends on complicated factors relating to (1) the level of trust we have in others,

(2) how we perceive another's acceptance of us, and (3) how we believe relationships outside the family may or may not be helpful in our distress. Deacon was moving *away* from people. Others, in their pain, may move *toward* people. For some persons, social and work relationships may become a significant support network which can aid in the traversing of troubled waters.

But there are those who find withdrawal much less threatening and also much more congruent with feelings of poor self-esteem. After all, they reason, how could someone *really* care or be concerned for another person who is quite worthless? And does the worthless person really want another person to see that worthlessness? Certainly not. Such a revelation to another would be clearly repulsive to that person and would probably result in rejection, with a further eroding of any remaining self-respect in the person who risks the self-disclosure. Thus, the best strategy is to pull back into increasing isolation.

Then there is the matter of judgment, or decision making. Difficulty in making even relatively simple decisions is another symptom of internal psychological conflict. As an individual becomes more dysfunctional, decisions having major consequences become almost impossible to make. Repeated indecision often creates much frustration for family, friends, and colleagues. Self-consciousness regarding decision-making problems further enhances the self-perception of inadequacy and incompetency, which contributes to a further tightening of the selective-negative-thinking net.

ANDERSON:

One thing has always separated me from most of my professional peers. I believe in God. This is not a shallow belief. It is something I specifically addressed and thought through a long time ago and something I constantly review.

I believe God exists, that he created all that exists, that he is good personified and that in him resides no evil whatever, that he desires and has made provision for a personal relationship with individuals in and of his creation. I believe that the only way mere man could ever have any contact with his truly sovereign God, and thus come to understand why humankind exists, is if God chooses to intervene in earthly affairs and reveal himself in terms people can understand. And I believe he did just that in Jesus Christ.

I also believe God knows and cares about what happens to each person. That's why it is so very frustrating not to *see* more direct evidence of God's involvement in my circumstance. Frustrating, but understandable. How can I blame him for not wanting to be even covertly involved in my life when even I don't much care for it? After all, the significant others of my life either do now or will shortly think of me as a loser. Why should God waste his time or energy on me? I don't doubt God's interest in my affairs. What I doubt is the here-and-now efficacy of being a Christian.

Intellectually I deny this. I know better, but emotionally I believe that good things happen to good people. Good things haven't much happened to me, therefore, I am not a good person. At one time I had a lively, living faith, but now I am living on faith, with behavioral burdens and no payoff. There is not only little joy involved but no hope, nor even particular desire, for the future. Joy is not to be my lot in this world. I hope it will be in the next, but even this hope is beginning to ossify. Not that I think I won't have joy in heaven; quite the contrary. *I just don't care today.*

DR. RICHARD:

Deacon had come to a crisis in his spiritual life which can be crystallized in the following way: If God really did love and care for Deacon, why was he not more directly involved in the resolution of the significant personal problems in Deacon's life? Where was God in the midst of this gloomy, stressful life, anyway?

In answer to this type of crisis, some persons may dismiss God as really not being there at all, or at least as being impotent to do anything about personal struggles. Deacon came down on the side of recognizing that God was there, but he blamed himself for God's lack of involvement in his life—how could God really care about someone who was a loser? How could God care about a life that Deacon himself found so profoundly unpalatable? Deacon's serious self-esteem problem was infecting his faith. Unable to love himself, he could intellectually assent to God's love, but he really could not *experience* that love in a deep, inner part of his being.

Many are the Christians caught in emotional and psychological struggles who wonder why God does not move in some way to deliver them from their painful travail. They may confess sins, attend church, read the Scriptures regularly, and verbalize their problems and frustrations to fellow Christians. Of course, all of these activities may provide help, but they may not significantly ameliorate some persistent problems. How can we understand this state of affairs? Is the troubled Christian an offender who by his life is somehow blocking God's work in his inward being? In other words, is the Christian "not right with the Lord"? Many times Christians assume that they are the problem and go on a search to see what they are doing to block God's direct intervention into their lives. But, as in Deacon's case, such a search often does not produce answers or changes. Indeed, it only results in further self-recriminations, accompanied by a heavier burden of guilt.

Nowhere do the Scriptures clearly state that Christians are spared from calamities that commonly beset mankind —and that includes emotional and psychological disorders

as well as physical misfortunes. Furthermore, although we
are clearly forgiven for our sins, there is no statement regarding our being spared either from the consequences of
our own actions or from the consequences of the actions
of others. In fact, the well-known biblical phrase, ". . . for
whatever a man sows, that he will also reap" (Galatians 6:7,
RSV), points to what may be considered a basic principle
woven into the fabric of life. Nor is it clear that when one
becomes a new creation in Christ (2 Corinthians 5:17) that
the past with its attendant memories and current consequences will suddenly disappear or be changed.

In reflecting on the above observation, we may conclude
that while God is at work in a remarkable way in our lives,
we have no guarantee of protection from psychological
crises. We will not necessarily be delivered from the results
of our, or others', actions. And the past, with its memories
and consequences, will not disappear. Because of these
facts, Christians need to understand that if they are troubled
by recurring psychological difficulties, the approach of asking whether they are "right with the Lord," as a way of trying to understand why God does not directly intervene,
misses the mark. This approach is not based in reality.

What is being faced has nothing to do with "rightness
with God," but with the consequences of psychological
traumas which have occurred in the past, a past in which
there may have been a minimum of control over what was
done to us and for us, or expected of us. By moving beyond
"am I right with God?" we become free to look openly at
other possible sources of our emotional and psychological
difficulties. In no way does this mean that God is less
present in our lives. What it does mean, however, is that a
new avenue for God's working has been opened and that,
with the help of his Spirit, we may embark on a journey of
self-discovery and growth—a joint venture with God which
does have the power to heal, restore, and make whole.

ANDERSON:

Winter is tailing out now, and I have almost exhausted my energy resources. I have just about given up the diminishing hope for anything which could properly be labeled as life. I am merely existing. I am going to die. But, like a soldier who cannot run, it does not make sense to put a bullet through my head. That resolves nothing. If that is going to happen to me, let the other guy pull the trigger. Let God put the bullet through my head. To die now, when I am in pain, would make pain absolute to the end. I have just about given up hope. And anyway, circumstances will bring on the end certainly soon enough.

I'm no longer able even to fantasize that I will live through this war. I am going to die. It's just a matter of when. Obviously, and regrettably, the war is likely to drag on for a number of years.

Let's deal with the "just about." As long as there is life within me and a good God in the heavens, there is some fragment of a chance that my circumstance will improve. Crazy things do happen in this world. After all, who would have thought that a Vietnamese boat person would have one day won a million dollars in the California lottery? But real life ignored the unlikelihoods, and it actually happened. By some good fortune unrelated to my own doing, something *could* happen to make life a rich experience, but only if I'm alive.

There is also my Christian perspective on the value of a life, as well as the fact that I acknowledge God's valid and loving claim on my life. But I must admit these things really don't weigh much in my not making a decision to end my life. If I rule out that most distant and remote *hope* that something good *might* happen, taking my own life would be a considered option, and only at that point would I have to face the spiritual dimension of suicide.

More than that, we are "church-going folks," active in our

church. Think of it: What would Mary say to someone who was sympathizing with her because her husband killed himself? I can't bear the thought of that prospect, although with her competence, she probably would handle it pretty well. But even if Mary could make it, the effect of my death on our now grown children could be devastating. They might wonder if they had contributed to my demise. There could be repercussions in their lives for years.

Another impediment to suicide, if another is needed, is the effect it would have on the hundreds of people whom I have taught in my adult Sunday school classes, or on those who know me as an occasional contributor to Christian publications. I have taught, written, and believed that man is made in the image of God and that to gain some kind of advantage through the arbitrary taking of any human life— mine in this case—is wrong. As I see it, the only advantage of doing so would be the welcome cessation of pain, but I am not utterly convinced that the kind of pain that is mine would cease with death. I might well find new dimensions of pain in hell.

DR. RICHARD:

What does a Christian do when the pressures of life are overwhelming and suicide is not an option?

Thoughts of self-destruction flicker through the minds of many people at some time during their lives. However, serious thoughts of suicide often arise in the crucible of intense psychological pain *and* hopelessness. The experience of hopelessness is especially significant. When there appears to be *no way out* of an overwhelmingly difficult and oppressive situation, suicide comes to be seen by the sufferer as an increasingly desirable, and even rational, option which will provide ultimate escape and relief from an intolerable reality.

Suicide is also a profoundly hostile act. It is the last act of self-hate against oneself, often the finale in a series of self-destructive behaviors. It is furthermore an act of great hostility toward those with whom one is involved emotionally. The self-destruction of one's life leaves surviving family and friends with many unanswered questions and unresolved feelings, making it particularly difficult for them to go through a healthy grieving process. In addition, they suffer from the lasting memories and often endless recriminating questions about what might have been done or not done that would have prevented the suicide.

Yet Deacon had *hope*—hope that glimmered in a dark night of soul-numbing despair. Hope comes in many different forms. But basically it has one message: Things will get better, somehow, someway, if only one can endure the present nightmare.

For the Christian, faith, hope, and love are cornerstones for the living of life. However, for the Christian, hope extends far beyond the consideration of heaven as a final state for the blessed; it is seen as an affirmation of God's loving guidance and assistance in helping to bring about positive changes in our present lives. *God working* now, *in and through us, is the essence of Christian hope*. Even in the bleakest times, this hope can illuminate our inner selves. It can reassure us that God is still with us, even though he is so hard to comprehend; that God still cares, even though that caring may be very difficult to experience; that he will see us through our deepest valleys, even though the valleys seem endless. Deacon had that hope, and because of it, he lived to tell his story.

ANDERSON:

The other day I gave up on life.
I do not give up on God, wife, family, work, church. I give

up on me, on my life. I give up on receiving satisfaction from any exterior source, and there is no satisfaction within. Thus my decision could be stated as a decision to neither seek nor work toward *anything* satisfying in life.

A great dimension in this resignation is the abandoning of all intellectual pursuit. It requires the application of all of the resources of my brain to get me through what I face at any given moment. I live in a boring state of crisis. I am suffering from mental anorexia.

The process has become the thing. I am now a survivor. Life can throw every damned thing it will at me, and I will survive. I know the implication is at best a toughness that denies that life has quality and that sees the vicissitudes of life as set against survival. It is a stoic mind-set which looks to survival itself as the only justifiable and available reward there is in this life. I find that to be an empty reward. But it's the only reward there is for me.

The truth is, life has become a colossal bore. I no longer take an interest in anything. *I don't want anything. I don't seek anything. I don't wish for anything. I don't hope for anything. I look forward to nothing. Tomorrow will be the same as today, just slightly more unraveled, and so it will go until the end comes.*

I don't *want* to die, not because I'm afraid to die—although I probably am. I don't want to abandon my family. Granted, I feel like an aging cow taking in grain so I can be milked to provide the support for the family. *But this cow loves the family.* And they depend on me.

It appears, if death does not intercede, that I face about ten more years of work to no satisfying end—then retirement and unrelenting boredom. When finally work is no longer a viable option, I will probably withdraw from everyone. By then, the emotional crippling will have reached an advanced stage. I will stay at home and venture out only when I absolutely must—that final trip to the cemetery, for instance.

For the present I just work and sit and try my best not to think.

My body is alive, yet my brain is dead. Only the acts of breathing and eating keep me from the grave.

Who will deliver me from this body of death?

DR. RICHARD:

In trying to find some way of coping with his struggles, Deacon evolved a stoic resignation. Resignation results when one believes that no other options are actually available. Options *may* be available (as Deacon later found), but they are definitely not apparent to the resigned person. Resignation is often a result of feeling psychologically "trapped." *It can be a frightening and deeply discouraging experience to feel that one is not free to move beyond certain limiting parameters,* whether these parameters be at work, in the family, in avocational pursuits, or in the mind.

In some cases resignation takes the form of a relatively easy acceptance of the reality of certain aspects of one's self or of one's situation that will not likely change. But in other cases resignation takes a more destructive form to the self and blocks the possibility of positive personal growth. Such was Deacon's plight. He correctly surmised that continuing in this state of resignation would mean continuing in a state of "living death" until his physical body expired. But his faint flicker of hope was not in vain. A change came that he could not even have imagined. A surprise? Yes, most definitely. Peculiar? No, not really, especially when one considers how God works.

II.

THE QUEST

The search for an answer to despair

Who will deliver me from this body of death?

    —Romans 7:24, RSV

ANDERSON:

Who, indeed? No one, that's who. As I rattle around inside the cage that is me, I have come to understand that Christ entered into a *spiritual* reclamation program with me, one that will be consummated in the world to come. Between now and then I'm stuck with my lot. I'm here. That's that.

What I actually have—in a sense, what I'm fortunately saddled with—is an unshakable faith in God. It does me no good to try to deny him. Could I deny the sunrise by pulling the shutters and closing my eyes? Such puny denial is transcended by the immutable fact of the sunrise. God is God and I am me and that is that.

So I have a faith, but it is a faith that is without earthly meaning. I affirm God, but *I cannot find any here-and-now solace in a God who has nothing to do with my here and now.* In a sense I say to him, "Where are you when I need you?"—but only in a sense, because I don't blame him for not being active on behalf of someone like me.

33

My faith is not at risk. It is my mental state that is in jeopardy, and faith seems not to apply to my mental state.

To put it a little differently, *I am not without faith, but I am just about without hope for anything in this life.*

DR. RICHARD:

Where is God, really, in the complexities and struggles of our day-to-day existence? Is there truly any connection between correct doctrine and fulfilling, satisfying daily living? I have seen in my office many Christians who certainly have strong beliefs, who acknowledge Jesus Christ as Savior and Lord, but who are in an intense struggle, trying to grasp why their faith is not more powerful in helping to resolve ongoing emotional and psychological difficulties. Often they, too, believe that God does not intervene because something is wrong with them. Frequently there is a strong sense that God's help is not deserved.

Again, it is not a matter of having a faulty faith or of believing we are not deserving of God's healing hand, but rather a failure to achieve new understanding and to be open to new avenues through which God can work to bring healing. Deacon's state of mind resulted primarily from thinking and feeling in the same old patterns. It is very easy, I believe, for us to find ourselves stuck in familiar, even habitual, thought and response patterns which may well keep us from discovering the very paths which will lead to our healing and growth. These may be the paths which God is trying to show us, but which our inflexible thinking keeps us from discovering. Only when the pain becomes too great and the night seems darkest may we force ourselves to look beyond what we have known or tried. So many times, I have seen a crisis become the crucial turning point which propels an individual into a quest that leads him or her to a journey of self-discovery which results in coming to terms

with life on a whole new plane. Deacon had come to that
very point of crisis, and slowly but perceptibly he was beginning to consider some new alternatives for dealing with
his problems.

ANDERSON:

With my stress mounting and life becoming more te-
dious every day, a question may come to mind: Why
doesn't he go to a psychologist or psychiatrist? That would
be doing *something*.

The straightforward answer: I don't trust them, that's
why. I see psychologists to be the placebos of the healing
arts. "Lie down on this couch. Tell me why you hate your
mother. Pay me a hundred dollars, and you'll feel better in
the morning." If you can make yourself believe that, you
may think you feel better in the morning.

The psychologist has become an optometrist of the mind,
prescribing rose-colored glasses. He means well. He's trying to help. It is not that I doubt the sincerity of the psychologist. But common sense tells us a person can be sincere
whether he's wrong or right.

Psychology is a universe of tentative conclusions. There
are no facts, only theories which change with the seasons.
Science and psychology don't quite mix. If science is a
Rembrandt, psychology is a cartoonist. There is some com-
monality of form, but you stand in awe of the one and tend
to laugh at the other.

Even the best of the lot seem to be troubled people who
make their living off other troubled people. The psychologist may have some need to feel . . . well . . . Godish or
something, to feel superior. He can't make it in the business
world, and academia provides too anemic a living; so he
retreats with his leather couch to create his own little world
where he can be king.

I realize this sounds cynical, and I regret that because I'm really not cynical about psychologists in private practice. Skeptical, yes, because I see psychology as a rickety art form at best, with interesting but unreliable theories. Also, it can be harmful. I dislike mind games, and I don't want to entrust myself to those who make their living tinkering about inside the heads of other people. Psychology is a speculative art form, for no one *really knows* how the mind works. People are making a lot of educated guesses, but they are still *guesses*.

DR. RICHARD:

Yes, why not go to a psychologist or psychiatrist? I suppose many persons have asked the question and have felt most uncomfortable with the thought. The efficacy of psychological help is often questioned. What can it really do? Will it end up being more harmful than helpful? Many times I have heard Christians wonder if psychotherapy will cause their faith irreparable damage and negatively affect their relationship with God. There is also the fear, frequently expressed, of not wanting anyone "tinkering" with one's head. What unfortunate results might come from such an endeavor?

This kind of questioning reflects a general lack of understanding of psychotherapy and a lack of trust in the process as well as the psychotherapist. It is no wonder. Since psychology is such a latecomer in regard to the other sciences, and since the application of psychological understanding to human behavior is even more recent, many persons may question whether psychological practitioners can be effective. Furthermore, the variety of ways used to understand and change human attitudes and behavior appear multitudinous and at times contradictory.

Since these issues concern many persons contemplating professional psychological assistance, they are worth a further look. As with any helping profession, solid research and valid clinical experience developed over a period of time greatly increase confidence in various therapeutic interventions, whether they be applied to marital problems, parent-child conflicts, or individual growth issues. The *variety* of effective interventions is related to the levels of complexity inherent in human beings. An intervention which helps bring about change at one level may be inappropriate for effecting change at another level. The skilled psychotherapist is the one who knows which kind of intervention will be most helpful, keeping in mind the individual's unique problems and the goals of the treatment agreed upon by the therapist and client.

Psychology is no longer in the "dark ages." A large and growing body of knowledge plus a widening circle of clinical experience both point toward a developing consensus regarding effective interventions. It is no longer simply a matter of guesswork or trial-and-error procedures.

ANDERSON:

I don't need a psychologist. After all, there is nothing in particular the matter with *me*. I am a *victim* of circumstances I have no power to control. I was born into the wrong home. I had teachers who really didn't care. I wasn't physically strong. I had a poor memory. My bosses are thoughtless at best or back-stabbing at worst. They don't like me and want to replace me. "Things" are going wrong and the dissatisfaction with these things is eating away at my vitals, but that is the natural consequence of my experience.

But to go to a psychologist! Even if they are legitimate, I cannot bear the thought of allowing *anyone* to have an insider's prospect of how my mind works. I know I have a nasty, conniving, and jealous mind. It goes with the territory, but others don't need to know that.

One reason I don't want the real me to show is that I love the world and people, but I don't want them to get too close to me. There is an almost palpable rot in my life, one which would disgust others if they saw or smelled it. So, as carefully as I can, I remain downwind of others, ever jockeying for the downwind position, shifting with the wind.

DR. RICHARD:

As reflected in Genesis, chapter 3, human beings are notorious for passing blame to others. Adam blamed Eve for his actions and Eve blamed the serpent. The fact is that the task of dealing with difficulties in our lives lies squarely on our own shoulders. The "Devil made me do it" mentality is universally infectious and a great barrier to the ultimate resolution of problems and to our continuing growth and maturing process.

Deacon used a very common rationalization for his plight in life: "This is the way I am, and since I've always been this way, I can't do anything about it." It is an attitude of resignation to the inevitable, as if one were predestined to live out his or her life in the context of psychological misery.

In my practice I see many individuals who pose the question, Can I change longstanding patterns which have plagued my life? To this I consistently answer, yes, change *is* possible. If as a psychotherapist I did not believe that truth, if I were not committed to that truth, and indeed did not see change occur in people, I would take down my shingle and pursue some other line of work.

Significant change always involves a confrontation with one's self and often with important others in one's life. These confrontations involve hard work, risk, and usually mild to intense discomfort, which initially may seem as great as the emotional pain which motivated one to seek help in the first place.

There are many reasons for resisting change, not the least of which is the fear of becoming too close to anyone, lest that person perceive the "true" nature of the individual needing assistance. After all, that "true" nature may be repulsive to all who view it, including the client. It was this fear of exposure to another and to himself that strongly impeded Deacon from seeking help. Yet he knew deep inside, as many do, that help was needed. But he was uncertain how to go about obtaining it in a way which would not drastically heighten his anxiety over being intimately known.

ANDERSON:

I used to enjoy going to open houses just to see inside— the pictures; the book titles; the amount of dust on the books; the magazines lying around; evidence of hobbies, avocations, and vocations; what prominence the television set was accorded; the quality of a stereo and the kind of records or tapes the owner kept handy; whether or not there was a Bible and other religious writings; the taste in paintings; the general condition of the house, the yard, and the storage area. Seeing these things gave insights into the person who lived in the house.

The brain is a house I would like to know. I have become interested in studying its structure. I want to know how things get into the brain and about the exits, if they are different from the entrances. I want to know what happens to the information that finds its way into the brain. I want to know where the kitchen is relative to the living room, whether there is a lived-in family room or den.

This is *not* to flirt with psychology. We're dealing here with floor plans, not decorations. I need not probe into the kind of books that are housed in the library of my brain, nor look for clues to give insight into the person who lives in that house. That's okay in the houses of others, but not in my own.

I'm not even curious about the *content* of that cranial cauliflower, but I am interested in *how it works*. The brain is a mystery. Life a celestial black hole, there is a good measure of evidence that it's there, but its operation can't be seen. Trying to understand the brain in depth is something like guessing what's in a box of a given dimension. Your guess is as good as mine.

I have to do *something* with my brain. I can't turn the accursed engine off. It will idle and surge and throb and pant as long as it is fed its blood-fuel. Perhaps I can learn enough about how it runs to divert its incessant drive into a preoccupation which will fill its time, and mine, with harmless activity and thus make life tolerable.

DR. RICHARD:

When people have been hurting long enough and intensely enough, they become strongly motivated to seek *some* solution. Even though it may be only a partial solution, it is perceived as a step that will bring a degree of relief from emotional pain and discomfort. So Deacon found a path that would allow him to begin to look inside, *yet from a distance*. He could begin by making an "objective" study of how the brain works. But he continued to have great fear about examining the contents of that complex cranial organ.

There are many and varied ways that the journey toward finding help is initiated. Some will drop hints to friends and associates that all is not well and watch for a response. Some will outwardly express their depression or anxiety and wait for a response. Some will become ill with stress-related symptoms which impede their lives, and hope others will take note. But there are also those who are more open and direct with themselves and will frankly admit to a close family member or friend that they are in trouble and need assistance.

Whatever path is chosen in the move toward getting help, it frequently seems to be related to (1) the value which is placed on getting help from others and (2) not being afraid of what others may think.

ANDERSON:

After doing some reading, I have come to think I once had a very active right (creative) brain. Music, color, form, and literature once struck deeply responsive chords in me. A child's face, the patience and wisdom in an old face, a happy couple walking together enjoying each other's company, a well-turned phrase, the pink of a sunrise—any one of these could make my spirits soar. Even now there is something within me which percolates in response to these kinds of things, even in my gloomiest moments. I presume this indicates right-brain tendencies.

But wait. This goes against the grain of what I have come to understand about myself. I don't think of myself as dormant. I think of myself as dead. I am as I am—and that's it. But undeniably there is some harmonic that thrums deep inside me when I remember those things that make my spirits soar; and after all, a dying ember would not be dying if it was not alive. Maybe I am *not* "as I am." Something is going on, something that still responds to beauty, else how could I be having these thoughts? Can that be an expression of my right brain?

This gives a new dimension to a potential study of the brain. I would still like to know how it works, for the reasons stated. Could it be that there is a discrete inference, beneath the level of genuine hope, that in studying the brain I might find there is some fun left in life after all? *But that's silly. There is little hope, and I have almost no desire for the future.*

Still, I wonder if my right brain *might* have within it

the seeds of *new* hope for a tolerable future. Some of the writings on right-brain and left-brain differences refer to a psychological test which could possibly confirm that creative talent exists (or doesn't exist) within me. If it does and if I can find out that it does, there may yet be some fun and satisfaction in my future. If it doesn't or I can't access it, well, I won't be any worse off than I am right now. This is a no-lose situation.

Routine psychological testing is a mindless enterprise which keeps batteries of bureaucrats in corporate personnel departments off the welfare rolls. That's about the end of the good it does. Such tests bug me. They are so transparently easy to manipulate.

If a test for right-brainedness is not a revamp of the old test grind—if in taking the test I find that I simply cannot manipulate the outcome with pat answers—it might be of some value. Such a test, effectively administered, would give me a snapshot of how my particular brain works. Even if the snapshot were fuzzy, it would still give me something to think about, perhaps to work on. The whole prospect is kind of exciting.

Exciting! Nothing has been exciting to me in a long time.

Think of it. Deep within I may find something of substance, something that I can poke and probe and kick and stretch and contort and make evaluative decisions about. If I *can* find that substance, perhaps, just perhaps, I can reshape the unsatisfying mass that is me into something I could live with. It does give a tiny ray of hope for the future.

If I know more about the brain, I might come to some private understanding of why I do as I do, and what I can do to entertain myself until I die. Standing against my distrust of psychologists are a group of Christians with Ph.D.s in psychology or related fields who operate a clinic in the area. One of them, Edward Stambaugh II, Ph.D., is a specialist with a neuropsychological approach to right- and left-brain testing. It sounds tailor-made for my interests. I'll go for it.

DR. RICHARD:

Underlying one's journey toward getting help is a glimmer of hope—something deep inside which tells the individual not to quit. For the first time in many years, Deacon felt a stirring of excitement. Now new hope was infused into his growing hopelessness, and he made a decision that started a whole chain of events which affected his life far beyond anything he had ever dreamed.

Over and over again, I find that persons struggling with significant psychological problems come to decision points which are crucial to the resolution of their problems and ongoing development. The choice leading to resolution and growth does not lead down an easy path. It is often a path filled with intense self-encounter and anxiety-producing uncertainties resulting from the exploration of previously unknown psychological territory. The path is a risky one. Many times clients have expressed to me how *terribly difficult* it has been to leave the familiar—though ineffective and sometimes destructive—ways of coping with life in order to find new, unfamiliar, but far more satisfying and emotionally healthy ways of relating to themselves and others.

How we love the familiar! It represents security, even though it may be utterly blocking us emotionally. But to change means to begin throwing off the smothering security blanket of familiarity and start being open to new and fresh understandings of ourselves and our past, of others, and of God.

Deacon made an uneasy decision to start moving down what was for him "a road less traveled." So it is for anyone who is really serious about change—a decision must be made to "go for it."

ANDERSON:

The test was even more interesting than I had hoped, and the findings were intriguing. In a way they *were* snapshots of my mind as it appeared on the day of the test.

Near the end of the evaluation session, Dr. Stambaugh and I discussed one neon-like sentence in his written summation. "You must take care that you do not allow disappointment and frustration to create a depressive outlook in life for you, which can easily result in withdrawal from the real problems of the world into a world of substitute gratifications and goals." And the report closed one sentence later. "I wish you success and the strength necessary to assert your own needs as of equal value with the needs of those around you in enriching your life."

Dr. Stambaugh, as I recall, did not exactly recommend counseling, and he certainly didn't suggest therapy; but he did in a sense point out that I itched in a place I couldn't quite reach to scratch. So the session ended, and while it was encouraging, it did not supply me with the *concrete* things I could do to occupy my time.

DR. RICHARD:

Sophisticated neuropsychological *tests in the hands of a competent and trained examiner often have the effect of confirming aspects of ourselves that we already know.* But they also provide additional information about how our brain processes the data received through the senses and how it results in particular patterns of learning and expression. This, of course, has important implications for our educational pursuits, vocational choices, and interpersonal relationships.

In Dr. Stambaugh's report, Deacon noted a sentence that touched on an area beyond the strictly neuropsychological aspect of brain function. Reference was made to "a depressive outlook in life." This struck a very sensitive chord in Deacon. In this sentence a connection was made between an *emotional state* and a resulting *pattern* of behavior Deacon used to cope with this state. Thus, the testing became a vehicle that started to uncover the emotional side of Deacon's life, and this led to an increased desire for more information and awareness.

Once the decision is made to seriously travel the pathway of change, the details of the route are not predictable. Information and insights often come from places that we least expect. The important point is that in the change process we become increasingly open to hearing, seeing, and experiencing parts of ourselves and our lives that heretofore we have tried to ignore or rationalize. It is precisely the new openness which makes it possible to hear and thus process the fresh information and insights which lead to both internal and external change.

III.

THE ENCOUNTER

A confrontation with the possibility of God's working through the psychotherapy process

Yesterday I called a Christian counseling service and made an appointment. Through the very rough day at work, my mind with no little foreboding, kept thinking about what I had done. Was it the right thing? Was I just being dumb about this, too? Was it something that would just go away with time and unrelated to counseling? By the time I went to bed, I was very depressed.

—From Deacon Anderson's Journal, April 30, 1985

ANDERSON:

In all of the world there was no one in whom I could confide. My thoughts *never* found expression in conversation nor in letters. But on the occasion of beginning therapy, I decided I would keep some notes because I have a memory like water. Like a stone dropped in water, an event in my life makes a little circle in my memory, but it quickly ripples away to nothing. Things might come up, I thought, which might one day be worth reviewing. Without a memory to rely on, I needed some other quick reference device, so I frequently jotted down my impressions of a session with Bob, and called the folder my "journal."

Most of us, I suppose, have at one time or another kept a diary. I did on a couple of occasions, but not after I reached age ten. Not much of what happens in a typical day is of interest to anyone, including me. But more significantly, *I didn't want to remember anything that happened. I just wanted to forget the day, not memorialize it in ink.*

While I didn't know it then, my journal became a form of crisis diary. It was the *one* place where I was giving honest expression to how I felt about things. No one would ever read it (at least that's what I thought at the time), so I could really be me as I cataloged how I was experiencing life.

The quote cited at the beginning of this chapter is from the very first entry in my journal, an entry about dreams. The remainder of that first entry also has particular pertinence to my story. It is given now in its entirety because it records a pivotal moment in my life. It records the time when I came to understand that daily experiences which are hidden from our conscious life may be mirrored to a remarkable degree in our dream life. But that's not what made it pivotal. The *content* of the dream is what made it pivotal.

Until this moment I had thought dreams were just a distressing reminder that one hadn't eaten properly during the day. I did not much think of them as riddles, and if they were, they were so esoteric that no one could figure them out. They were gossamer eruptions of the nighttime mind. Only the mentally unstable would probe them for meaning. Dream interpretation was best left to the Bible and biblical times.

Besides, I hated my dreams. My dreams, like all else in my life, were terrifying and boring at the same time. I hated them.

Here, then, is my first journal observation:

> For years, many years, I have had an almost nightly dream of stifling frustration. While no two dreams were identical, all had the same theme and shared certain characteristics.

1. I was enroute someplace, but I was never quite sure where my destination was or why I was supposed to go there. It was important that I make my goal—I had no other option—but *why* it was important was never clear.

2. The route I was traveling was unusual, but then the circumstances in the dream were always unusual, and that made acceptable the bizarre nature of the route I was to traverse. Sometimes I found myself on steep mountain paths, sometimes at the beach with the sea rising, or in a rickety war-scarred building.

3. My "going someplace" *always* involved life-threatening peril.

4. Other people, sometimes one and sometimes many, were with me and were skilled in the techniques necessary for the journey. Blessedly they were always understanding of my predicament. My size or health or the light (or heavy) clothing I was wearing, or a sudden change in the circumstance made it reasonable that what they could accomplish easily was difficult, and likely impossible, for me. They never laughed at me, never were critical, and never coaxed me to give it a try. I did try, always, but only because I could not turn back.

5. When I made a safe transit through a perilous passage to apparent safety on the other side, I inevitably found I was not at my goal, but now faced a new and different peril before I could attain the goal. If I finally had the courage to jump off the high board, I found myself in sand instead of water, but the sand seemed to be quicksand—that kind of thing.

6. The dream did not end nor did it peter out. I always woke up in despair and terrible, terrible frustration. I could not win out, and I could not lose.

This dream had plagued me for thousands of nights, *literally* thousands of nights. Not once did I succeed in meeting and conquering the last obstacle, in gaining my goal. On countless days I literally shuddered to consciousness, spent and depressed, exhausted before the day had begun.

Yesterday I called a Christian counseling service and made an appointment. Through the very rough day at work, my mind with no little foreboding, kept thinking about what I had done. Was it the right thing? Was I just being dumb about this, too? Was it something that would just go away with time and unrelated to counseling? By the time I went to bed, I was very depressed.

Last night, for the first time in my life, I had the "frustration" dream and made it through to the end. After a long series of not terribly difficult traverses, I came to a small door. The door was open, and I saw a ladder which reached from our level down to a floor a very far distance below.

Mary was with me. The others, whom we did not know, had all gone down the ladder before me. The place where we stood was a rooftop with nothing whatever in view except the floor and the wall with the small door in it. Somehow I knew it was not possible for us to retrace our steps, to go back to where we had come from, wherever that was.

As I checked out the ladder, I found it was not only shaky, but it had rungs missing, several in a row, and it had oddly shaped and threatening metal straps with razor-sharp edges. I would have to either slip under or climb over the straps to descend the ladder. That the ladder did not have the straps the others had gone down was an unexplained given. Now I saw that the ladder stopped a couple of inches short of the bottom of the door. It was not fixed to the wall but just leaned against it. As I first tested my weight on it, the ladder slipped to the left several inches and I hooked it with my foot and pulled it back into place.

There were people at the bottom of the ladder who were watching with no particular interest. No one said anything, to me or to each other. They just watched without interest.

I realized this was it. Either I was going to go down that ladder, or I was going to be forever stuck where I was.

I resolved to go down the ladder, even if it meant that the ladder would fall and I would be killed. (It never seemed to occur to me that I might only be hurt.) Without telling Mary,

I seemed to indicate to her that I was going, and she, without giving any outward signs, seemed to understand. Now those who had been watching at the bottom of the ladder faced away from the wall against which the ladder rested, and thus away from the ladder. It seemed then and seems now unusual, but for some reason it made sense at the time.

At that moment, a woman was on our level, and she said something like, "He's coming," and nodded or pointed to a large, hideous apparition shuffling toward us. He was in old, rough clothes. His eyes were closed, and his face was like an evil mask. I was not sure if he was coming for me or if he would simply shove me aside and go down the ladder. I was only sure of one thing—he was evil.

When the woman called him to my attention, most of my weight was on the ladder. For a second I thought of pulling myself back through the door and onto the roof. For one second I could not desert Mary in this awful moment, but then I realized the evil man was interested in some fashion with me and would not harm nor even take note of her. Maybe there was some way of escape. But again, I realized, this was it. I did it now or I would never do it.

Whether I said it or thought it, I don't know, but at that last moment of decision, I think I said, "The hell with it," and committed myself to the traverse.

The very next moment I was on the ground and maybe fifty feet away from the ladder. I was not yet at my goal, at my destination, whatever that was, but it was now a forgone conclusion that I would walk easily to that point. I called out to Mary, "I made it! I made it!" She shared my joy and, apparently without having to climb down the ladder, was immediately next to me.

We looked up to see if the evil man was coming, and instead of him, we saw a number of men in their early twenties who ran to the top of the ladder and stood up straight as they ran down the rungs, almost skiing down them. They were incredibly skilled, but did not seem to enjoy the romp. Instead, they seemed almost disinterested, like zombies. I thought they were collectively the evil man. They came very fast and very close together, and then continued walking at that fast pace off to the left, never making contact with us, not even eye contact.

I woke up then, utterly exhausted and even breathing hard, both from fright and great joy. As I stirred about in bed, Mary also stirred, and I found she was at least partly awake. "I made it," I said quietly, "I won." She knew exactly what I was talking about.

DR. RICHARD:

Dreams—those mystifying and often emotionally stirring sleep experiences—really do afford us a candid look into our unconscious minds. However one wants to conceptualize the unconscious, there is no question that there are memories as well as current fears, wishes, and conflicts that are outside of our present awareness. Dreams are a way that our mind has of bringing parts of the unconscious to consciousness. Everyone has dreams, and sleep research has shown that dreams are apparently very important to healthy emotional and mental functioning. Dreams occur both when we are falling into a deep sleep and when we are coming out of it again. We may be in and out of deep sleep several times during our sleep cycle; thus we may recall dreams that occur at various times during the night. However, most people tend to recall dreams which occur in the final sleep cycle, near the morning. Not all people remember dreams well, but this can be improved through a deliberate effort and commitment to write down dreams shortly after they have been experienced.

A helpful way to understand the meaning of dreams is to approach them as a scenario which uses *symbols* as a primary means of expression. One of the reasons people have so much trouble understanding their dreams is that they try to interpret them literally when dreams speak symbolically.

The persons, places, and activities viewed in the dreams usually represent someone or something else. Of course, the meaning of some dreams is quite obvious and apparent to the dreamer, while the meaning of other dreams is much more obscure, and one must have a fairly good self-awareness already to make sense of them.

Repetitive dreams, such as the one which plagued Deacon for years, always are connected to ongoing, deeply unresolved fears or conflicts. In Deacon's case he had repetitive dreams which symbolized his incredibly profound confusion over the direction of his life, as well as great fear over making a journey toward any dimly understood goal. Furthermore, the dreams also testified to his fear that once the goals were achieved, they really would not make any difference in his life. Thus intense feelings of despair and frustration welled up after such dreams.

The dream that Deacon had subsequent to contacting my office is an excellent example of how new and awakening expectations change one's internal mental life. While the dream had all the elements of the previous dreams, this one was significantly different because this time Deacon "made it." It was also significant because it showed that Deacon had come to a turning point in his life and, in spite of all his fears and reservations, committed himself to a course of action that now was giving him hope. Indeed, even before the first counseling session, the dream revealed he was beginning to move away from despair toward hope. He woke up frightened but with "great joy." Even the part of him that focused on self-destruction (represented by the "evil man") was being rendered impotent.

Often the decision to enter therapy brings renewed hope. I have seen this experience in many of my clients. A turn in the path has been made and the potential for something new to emerge is there. In short, there is *hope,* and hope is to the psychological life as air is to the physical—necessary for survival.

ANDERSON:

The First Visit

Dread contested with hope on the first drive to the counseling offices. From the moment the appointment had been fixed, I had second and third and fiftieth thoughts about the idea of consigning my head to another person.

There were periods of fundamental concern about the validity of the course I was taking, but there was no backing away from it. I had decided to have at least an initial conversation with the psychologist, and that I *would* do. But my unease was manifested in my self-talk. I said to myself that I had to live ever after with the consequences of other dumb decisions I had made in my life. *This one may not pay off*, I thought, *but at least it won't be a public embarrassment—only my wife knows about it, and she supports it.*

The commitment to act did not put an end to the questions, but for every question that burbled into my consciousness, something seemed to rummage about in the dark recesses of my mind to find some kind of an answer.

Do I really need this? *I really need something to reverse the course of my life.*

Can *anyone* do anything about my situation? *I won't know if anyone can help if I never risk letting someone try.*

Is Bob Richard the right person for the job? *Bob is a person known to me by acquaintance and reputation, a psychologist familiar with and friendly to Scripture.*

Could I not spend the money better on other things? *"Things" no longer give me pleasure as it is.*

How badly will it hurt? *I don't know. I do know the pain can't be worse than what I'm now experiencing.*

If something goes wrong, will I be worse off than I am now? *I will be increasingly worse off if I don't go.*

Isn't this all a figment of my imagination? *My problems are not imagined.*

Is the investment worth it? *Any relief whatever will be worth it. Even to know nothing can be done about my pain will be better than wondering if I could be helped.*

Have I got enough time left in life to make this worth it? *At fifty-six, most of my life is over. I wonder whether therapy is worth the investment of time and money. I don't know.*

Is it too late to get involved with therapy? *I don't know. My mind has set like Jell-o, and I just don't know if it can be liquefied and remolded with significant change. It is not too late for my life to end like a rancid dishrag, that is for certain. Perhaps there is some chance it could end on an upbeat.*

Even while the debate plunged relentlessly on in my head, I recognized with specific clarity that I wasn't in need of an oil change and a lube job. I didn't need to get along a little better. Either I needed an overhaul or I needed nothing at all. The time for playing games was past.

"Games" doesn't do justice to the bargaining that was going on inside. I was flirting with interminable death. That is not an exaggeration. I was facing the loss of interest in everything. Even with the compelling family interest, I had to wonder about the value of going on living. That was one half of my mind set as I drove down Highway 680 to my appointment.

The other half of my mind flirted with hope, or maybe with "wish." I wanted the overhaul. I wanted not to be who I now was. At a minimum, I knew my mental health was *dis-eased.* I suspected that there was some part of me which was imprisoned by my mind-set and which wanted more than anything else in all creation to break out of the bonds which held it, some part of me which had no means of expression in life, a shred of sanity which got clobbered every time it tried to make its feelings known. I *thought* quite strongly that I would like that part of me, perhaps as much as I disliked the person I was.

This hope was in mortal combat with something else, the total absence of confidence that *anyone* was qualified to untangle the Gordian knot that I had worked all of my life to untie with such disastrous results. God could have done it with a snap of his fingers, couldn't he?

Even as I drove, the idea of not showing up—just skipping the whole thing—surged through my mind. There were moments when I was sure there was really nothing at all wrong with how I faced life; a little willpower exerted here, a little backing off there, and everything would be fine. But then I would realize that such thoughts were deadly games I was playing with my life, trying to pull the rug out from under that part of me which wanted to find expression.

As I sat in the reception room, my mind raced through a thousand disparaging things I had said about psychologists: people who shared their mental instabilities with others for a fee, the lost leading the blind, wackos, professional nuts, brain disordered, people who are self-centered in the extreme, the pretend society with the pretend language for pretend illnesses, those who prefer to listen for a living rather than work, the human poodles of an affluent society, unstable practitioners of an unreliable art, the gurus of the ascetic, mind mashers, social wobblies.

Offsetting this attitude was a remarkable experience in my own home. I had seen Mary blossom from a beautiful, competent, somewhat officious and unassertive person to one who learned she could enjoy being who she was, that she had a right to her own opinions and to the expression of them. I had seen such a positive and wonderful turnaround in Mary through her exposure to psychological training that the changes were utterly undeniable. Indeed, if it had not been for those changes and for the fact that Mary was taking courses to become a lay counselor, I would not even be in the reception room.

From her volunteer work as a lay counselor, Mary had shared with me a number of stories of lives warped by circumstances much worse than mine. Yet through therapy, they were coming out of the shadows of despair and into the light of day. Their lives had been improved in varying degrees from better to dramatically changed. The evidence was irrefutable. There *had* to be something to it. Mary and her clients, who were unnamed and unknown to me, were living witnesses to the effectiveness of therapy.

Not everyone benefited, I remembered. Some dropped out. But in discussing these cases with Mary, I noted that progress was made by those who *chose* to make progress, by those who stuck with it. The logical conclusion was that those who did not make progress, who did not experience some degree of relief from the pressures that brought them to therapy, *elected* not to improve. They chose what they were familiar with over what might be. Without going into why they so chose, it was apparent that therapy had given them a new option—which they had rejected.

That was why I was waiting to see Dr. Robert Richard. He was a psychologist in private practice, an ordained minister, and a founder of the lay counseling center where Mary got her training and did volunteer work. The purpose of the center was to treat people whose income prohibited them from receiving professional care. They paid what they could, if they could. Bob and his professional Christian peers sought to extend the benefits of counseling to people who otherwise might never have a chance to receive urgently needed treatment. That attitude said something to me.

And there was the matter of spiritual life. I am satisfied there is a God who has revealed himself in Jesus Christ. My life is centered around this fact. I could not relate to a psychologist who based his life on anything other than a fundamental connection with his Creator. Nor could I take a psychologist who saw my religious understanding as a quirk in thinking.

On the other hand, I could not abide discussing my life with a Christian psychologist who did not *think*, who was so dogmatic in his understanding of life that he could not appreciate my problems and my perspective. At this moment more than forgiveness and most certainly more than guilt assigned, I needed to gain understanding.

I needed a tough psychologist, one I couldn't bully or shuck. I could not abide someone who was smarmy and unknowingly dishonest in his desire to help me.

I needed a brain, a truly bright and educated person who could fathom the complexities of my problems which had been so long abuilding. He, or she, had to be tough and sharp and honest and self-confident. I didn't need sweet and kindly advice.

I had become acquainted with Bob Richard when I took an assertiveness training course from him, more to please Mary than for any other reason. I attended with her. It was interesting and not without benefit, but in retrospect, the greatest benefit was that it allowed me to get to know Bob a little and to trust him a little.

DR. RICHARD:

Even as Deacon drove to my office, he continued to wage a battle within. But when he was honest with himself, he knew he had made the right decision (and, in his dream, his unconscious confirmed this). An important part of his decision to go ahead and come was the knowledge of his wife's positive growth experience as a result of her lay counselor training and work, plus his knowledge of me through his wife and through an assertiveness training workshop I had given.

Very often the best recommendation one can have for psychotherapy is to talk with someone who has experienced it or who at least has had exposure to it. Such a person is often able to reduce the prospective client's fears and doubts by giving a realistic picture of the therapy process. This helps destroy potentially disturbing fantasies.

Furthermore, knowledge of the therapist's reputation as well as some previous positive contact with the therapist in another setting may help raise the initial trust level.

ANDERSON:

Bob's smile was friendly and warm and his handshake firm as he invited me into his office. I'm not sure what I had expected, probably a couch and some dramatic lighting. What I hadn't expected was a quiet, tastefully decorated, informal office looking out on an attractive public patio. There were two comfortable chairs in a restful green plaid and a larger recliner in black. I took one of the green chairs, my back to the window, and Bob took the other. I took that chair so no one going past the window could recognize me.

It is not easy for me to describe the first session. I was exceedingly nervous. Bob was pleasant enough and not intimidating, but I was intensely aware that I was being sized up or evaluated. My mind was kind of whirling and skittering, not able to settle on anything and unable to tolerate even a few seconds of silence.

My journal notes following the first visit show that "we talked in general about how I experience life." I was almost desperate for Bob to know that the problems with my feelings were not short-term; they "are, for most purposes, lifelong," I said. The urgency was present because I was afraid Bob thought I might have come in for counseling, which I later learned is almost by definition short-term and behavior-specific. I didn't know that, and I was too scared to muster up whatever it took to state outright that I came for therapy. Perhaps I still wasn't certain therapy was right or necessary.

Was I just supposed to talk to him? Was he supposed to ask me questions? I didn't know the "rules," and I could not endure silence, so I filled up the time with talk. I said I would not go to a non-Christian psychologist because we would have essential differences in the fundamental understanding of life. Thus, I said, they "are less credible advisors." Bob took my statement at face value and noted that as Christians we don't really believe in "flukes." We believe in the presence of God in our activities; we are not alone. We who are Christians understand we are known to and loved by God, and that he takes singular interest in our circumstances.

I even told him that I came to the session with reservations. But I also told him that I was now of the opinion that psychology in the hands of a Christian is a powerful tool which can help us understand ourselves. I left it that open-ended.

Then I said, "So, if I understand why I am as I am, what is the value of that understanding? Does understanding that I have just broken my arm make my broken arm become well, or hurt less? I have long thought that time is not only the best healer but is perhaps the *only* healer of wrong thinking, but in my case, it isn't working. Things have gotten perceptibly worse, and I seem to be running out of time."

Something inside me would not let me say outright: "I need help. I'm dying. I need long-term treatment and help."

I didn't have to. My journal entry for that day goes on to say, "Without my having brought it up, Bob noted that he would like to spend a number of sessions learning more about how I perceive the world about me and how I came to those perceptions."

No one can ever know what effect that statement had on me. I had half expected to be told I had no real problem, and thanks for coming. I had half expected to be told my problem was too great to really take up at this age, and thanks for coming. I had half expected to be told I didn't have anything really wrong but I could come back a few times to talk about things. In this instance, three halves made a very black hole.

How I perceived the world and how come I perceived it that way—the differentiation between how I *saw* the world and how the world might actually *be* thundered home to me. Perhaps the world as I understood it did not exist. There was nothing insulting in his statement, no innuendo that I was unbalanced or unusual. It was more an unemotional observation that it was possible I saw the world differently than it actually was.

Maybe I was like the child who couldn't reach the stone on the bottom of the swimming pool because the refractions of the water had distorted the distances. There was nothing *wrong* with the child; things were simply not where they appeared to be. But again, *what good would it be to know that I perceived the world wrongly*, if indeed I did? I had developed the systems necessary to get along in the world *as I saw it*. Knowing that I perceived it wrongly seemed to solve nothing.

Even as these things were buzzing around in my hypersensitive mind, Bob said something that made eminent good sense to me. "After I get a handle on how you perceive the world, we can address the matter of interventions."

DR. RICHARD:

When I first shook hands with Deacon Anderson in the waiting room and led the way to my office, I immediately recalled his presence in my assertiveness training class a few years earlier. Deacon struck me then and now as a tall, nice-looking, warm, and pleasant man in his fifties. In my office he began to talk about those things that prompted his visit. He touched on numerous concerns, including his repetitious dreams (he also shared the dream where he "made it"), frustrations at work, a deep feeling of inadequacy, a tendency toward social withdrawal, periods of intense depression, problems with memory, and he alluded to a very unhappy childhood. Based on some of his remarks, I noted that he might be blocking out whole segments of early childhood experiences.

The first session is very important for both client and therapist. In the first session I try to get an overview of what is going on in the client's life, and I also try to develop a strong sense of rapport and trust by using therapeutic listening skills. It is only after a positive and trusting relationship between therapist and client has been established that *any* meaningful counseling or psychotherapy can take place, no matter how skillful the therapist may be at applying particular interventions. During the first session the client's verbal self-disclosure—as well as non-verbal behaviors such as posture, facial expressions, and gestures—tells me how well the client is functioning mentally and emotionally.

The first session is also very important from the client's point of view. It is usually that first session which becomes the prime impetus to return for a further session. Often, as with Deacon, there is much uncertainty about what will be discussed or what will happen. Most people begin to relax as the session progresses, and I give the session some structure by saying what I hope we can cover, reflecting empathically on their statements and asking clarifying questions.

Often, if the first session is successful, people leave having experienced something of value. In Deacon's first session, he experienced two very important insights. First, he recognized that I believed a number of sessions would be needed to help him, and thus I was sensitive to the fact that *his problems were not just surface matters.* Second, he saw that *his perceptions of himself and the world might be distorted.* That *I* saw he might have distorted perceptions had a major initial impact on Deacon. But, as he asked, "What good would it do simply to understand that one may be perceiving the world wrongly?" After all, an adjustment had been made to living with the perceptions, whether they corresponded accurately to the world or not.

ANDERSON:

Interventions

My journal entry for that first session notes, "To intervene is to deliberately do something from outside to take control over a circumstance which otherwise would continue to exist." The grammar leaves a lot to be desired, but it was written in the heat of discovery.

This is what it meant to me: I had over the years tried everything I could try—from prayer to drinking and back —to change the way I perceived the world. Everything had failed. If anything was going to be effective, it would have to come from outside me; but it had to meet with my approval before it could do its work.

Bob seemed to be proposing that he would study my vision to see why the stone on the bottom of the pool seemed to me to be at a particular place when it was actually at another and that he would work with me to design a pair of glasses that would enable me to see things as they really existed. It wasn't until much later that I came to see he was helping me remove the glasses which caused the distortion of my natural vision.

DR. RICHARD:

I often explain to clients at the conclusion of the first session that before anything can be done about their problems (that is, before any intervention can be made), time must be spent understanding how an individual currently sees him- or herself and the world, and also how he or she came to these perceptions. In other words, what thinking, feeling, and behavioral patterns have developed over time which have blocked the individual's ability to engage in on-going positive psychological development. Understanding these patterns and how they developed is crucial to both the therapist and the client. Once such understanding does occur, it forms the basis for making decisions about what interventions should be used to change patterns—which in turn will bring healing and free the individual to move down the path of psychological growth and health. Deacon colorfully described the process with his metaphor of eyeglasses and distorted vision. Ultimately, for Deacon it was a matter of getting rid of those glasses that had distorted his vision.

ANDERSON:

A Second Look at Dreams

Earlier we observed that I disbelieved in the value of dreams. A second look would now shed new light on the therapy experience.

At best, I thought dreams were like the emergency vents on an old-fashioned pressure cooker. When things got too bad and the head of steam built up to a dangerous level, a thoroughly rotten dream would help to clean out the mental pipes. *How* that worked—in truth, *if* that worked—was a real question for me. But as we have seen, therapy had not even started when dreaming became of more than passing interest.

Who was trying to tell me something was up for grabs: My subconscious mind? God? Something or someone else? I didn't know, but somehow almost all of my dreams immediately began to give powerful insights into what was going on in my mind. The following dream is a sample of how dreaming can contribute to understanding.

Kidnapped

The dream began with Mary and me returning to a church day school or nursery to pick up a son, who was two or three in the dream. When we entered the small home that served as that day-care center, we saw that all the other parents had retrieved their kids, but our son was gone. When we had left him, he was standing on a table smiling at us, and now he was simply gone.

The women attending the center were not at all helpful, partly because they were also bewildered and partly because they were embarrassed that this had happened. "We notified the authorities as soon as we saw he was gone," one said, "but nothing has happened since then."

There are no words which can describe the depth of the sadness that possessed me at that moment. It was devastating. But I rose above my despair and became frantic in my resolve to find my son—frantic bordering on panic.

We quickly learned there were about three thousand people in the town. Mary and I decided that we would immediately take eight-by-ten photographs of our son and separately canvas every house in the town, asking if the householder had seen him. We would mount the pictures on paint-mixer spatulas so they could be held up shield-fashion directly in front of the householder. We would carefully watch their eyes for any signs of recognition, and at the slightest suggestion of it, we were going to push past the householder and search the house.

At this point I woke up feeling profoundly sad.

As I thought of the ramifications of the dream and associated it with my current circumstance, I began to see that the little boy who was never seen in the dream was not my son but was me as a child. The child I was at one time just disappeared at about that age and never appeared again.

As I wrestled with this implication, I found myself becoming very angry at whoever would cause or allow something like the disappearance of a child to happen.

Late that day I wrote, "It is now eight hours later, and I'm still mad and sad."

Someone else who never was a child took the child's place. That someone else was a tremendous actor because he fooled everyone who knew the missing little boy. They didn't realize that the original boy was gone. The prince was gone and a pauper, an impostor, had taken his place.

What had happened to the original boy? The dream suggested strongly that the child was not dead but was missing. Thus, very early on in therapy I had dredged up from deep within me a first hint that the seeds to the solution of the problem that faced me were within my mind, reachable now only in the state of sleep, but with the help of Bob, these notions might come closer to the surface of thought.

With this dream and others like it, I came to appreciate that there was some other intelligent part of me which desired to help me come into a healthy way of thinking. It was undeniable. Something was operating at another level and making connection with my conscious mind through the means of dreams. I know it sounds a little schizophrenic, doesn't it, or weird. But there was nothing schizophrenic or weird about it. It was very matter of fact and straightforward.

The Dream As a Parable

Christ frequently taught in parables, but he did not leave those he loved baffled by the riddle. He explained it. I found myself now viewing dreams as parables, and parables without explanations are of little use. My earlier dreams maybe *had* acted as a relief valve for my emotions because what was inside me had no other escape. But now I entered into an enormously rich parable life.

Now I, who could never remember any dream except the living nightmare, could remember dreams in vivid detail. I cannot explain it, nor do I understand much about the source of the dreams. Neither do I have any sophisticated understanding about how an airplane flies. But both dreams and airplanes work.

My assumption that there had been some kind of abrupt

cutoff of childhood was affirmed in a second and completely different dream three weeks later.

Idyllic Isle

In this dream I took Mary and one of my sons to a Pacific island to show them where I had been brought up just prior to the war. In the dream my dad was a missionary to the tiny Polynesian population, and my childhood had been idyllic until the war started.

The Japanese military came, but we were not perceived to be any threat to the war effort and we were not hassled by the occupation army. In fact, I was treated very well by both the Japanese and the natives, who were a kindly people.

When I turned twelve and my brother turned seventeen, I began to worry. My brother would be susceptible to the draft in a year, with me to follow a few years later. I was quite sure the Japanese simply could never let my brother and me live to reach fighting age.

The tenor of my life made an abrupt 180 degree turn. Suddenly every moment, waking and sleeping, was filled with terror. The enemy would one day decide to kill me, and I knew if they didn't do it at this moment, they would do it another day. I lived in constant terror in this lovely, beautiful island surrounded by a loving and kindly native population.

The beginning of this dream is described in the following journal entry.

As soon as we landed, I began to cry because I recognized so much of what was around. There were no natives nor Japanese on the island now. Everywhere I turned, there were old memories I had forgotten, and I would begin to cry quietly at every one of them.

It became time for us to go, and it was very sad because I didn't really want to leave. I wanted to be small again, and to live here with Mary and my son, but without the terror. I wanted to live there as I am today, but sort of take up where I left off.

Again I began to weep for how tragic things were during the war, what an idyllic life had been so close to reality and had been missed . . . forever.

It came time to leave. It was so hard to leave. I wanted to stay there with Mary forever, but we had to leave and that, too, made me sad. I suppose that was because I thought we would never return again. I could not quit weeping. The tears flowed and flowed.

Dream settings usually have nothing to do with historical reality. My father was never a missionary, I have never been on a Pacific island except Hawaii, and I have no brother. But dreams have a reality all their own, and it isn't the least bit less true than our "real" world. They portray with pinpoint accuracy part of what is going on inside us.

Here, as in the dream of the kidnapping, terror replaced an ideal childhood. One moment everyone was kindly and loving, and the next moment the lad who had responded with such delight to that treatment was gone forever, replaced by a boy who was terrified in the night and in the day.

Bob helped me to understand that the dream was true, that I *was* terrified as a youngster and that there was part of me yearning to go back and pick up my life at that point where innocence gave way to survival instinct. Can one go back? Can a person in his mid fifties rethread the needle and start sewing again?

DR. RICHARD:

It was during the sixth session that I began to look more closely at Deacon's dreams. Prior to this I was getting to know Deacon, at least on the surface. His struggles with low self-esteem, his lack of interest in life, his easy discouragement, his social withdrawal—all were obvious. But it also became apparent that through dreams, Deacon was allowing himself to come into contact with unconscious aspects of himself. Not only was he able to remember his dreams, soon he was succeeding in writing them down in a way that facilitated their communication to me and thus made an important contribution to my, and Deacon's, understanding of his subconscious thought processes.

While dreams were very confusing to Deacon, he sensed that they carried some very important messages from one part of himself to another. He was correct. For truly the dreams offered the first early glimmer that something had been very wrong in his childhood. Not only did the dreams point symbolically to early childhood trauma, but the emotions that accompanied the dreams were further confirmation of the intensity of his childhood experiences. Following the dream where his "son" was lost, Deacon felt both sad and mad. The dream of terror on the idyllic isle brought tears of sadness, especially when it came time to leave. There was a great sense of loss connected with the leaving, but also a strong sense of wanting to take up where he had left off, to relive the idyllic isle experience, but without the terror.

It was clear to me that for healing to occur at a significant level, that is, for change to occur which would be far reaching and enduring, we would have to probe Deacon's past at some length to find that "child" which had become terrorized and lost to conscious awareness.

It is very common for persons who have had a traumatic childhood to remove from awareness many of the painful and sad memories associated with their upbringing. In fact, some people have so totally repressed specific experiences that they are unable to bring to consciousness certain very significant events which may have helped shape their later psychological and emotional functioning. This is particularly true in the area of child abuse, either physical, sexual, or both. The repression process is not done consciously, but appears to be a major way the mind has of automatically protecting itself against intense emotional pain or conflict.

Repression has long been recognized as a major defense human beings have developed in coping with life. While it serves a very useful purpose in protecting us from unwanted and painful memories, repression also can be a major block in helping us get to those painful memories which are still "alive" and emotionally charged—memories which remain out of our awareness, but which betray their existence by occasional and sudden intrusion into our lives.

Such intrusions may be seen in dreams, but they also may be seen when we find ourselves overreacting emotionally in unpredictable and inexplicable ways to certain events and relationships in the here and now. Irrational fears, unusual suspicions, outbursts of anger, waves of sadness, feelings of remorse or melancholy which come upon us for no obvious reason *may* be the result of a current event or relationship's triggering an unconscious memory and evoking feelings surrounding that memory. Since we are unaware of the connection, the emotions we experience seem not to "fit" the current circumstances.

For persons who have largely repressed important but painful memories which are still actively intruding on their lives, the questions the therapist must face are these: how does one really uncover these memories, that is, bring them to consciousness; further, once that is done, how can the emotions surrounding these memories be "discharged" in a way that renders them impotent so they no longer have a negative effect on the individual? In short, how can traumatic and disruptive elements from one's past be brought from the unconscious to the surface and dealt with so that a deep and lasting healing may occur?

Increasingly in my practice I was coming to see that, while change could and did occur for many persons through rational, cognitive-oriented techniques, there is a large group of persons, including Deacon, who have to find change at a much more profound level. To help bring about change at this level, many therapists use a form of regression therapy which puts individuals directly in contact with memories of their repressed past. Regression therapy, more than any other intervention I know, helps surface repressed memories and bring about healing, thus freeing the client from years of negative intrusions while also providing *the basis for a new perception of the self*. I knew such an approach would ultimately be needed for Deacon *if* he committed himself wholeheartedly to the psychotherapy process.

ANDERSON:

Truth and the Perception of Truth

Dreams aside, Bob and I were already working together to see life as it existed apart from how I perceived it. I had had some measure of career success which I attributed to "dumb luck." But Bob saw my attribution as irrational when compared to the consistent evidence over many years. I began to wonder about it myself.

Already there were little evidences that things were changing. When I came to Bob, I had all but lost my ability to focus on things. I have described how my mind seemed so fragmented I couldn't concentrate on anything for more than a few seconds. But now I found a new or renewed ability to focus on things I liked to do, at times sustaining interest without effort for hours at a time.

This had inadvertently confirmed the right-brain/left-brain test finding of "no incapacitating difficulty" in handling ideas. I thought about this and discussed it with Bob at our next meeting. My journal entry after the meeting reads in part:

Some things I do not catch on to for neurological reasons, but some things I don't catch on to for psychological reasons, there existing a kind of psychological filter in my brain which inhibits accepting the information for what it is. This, Bob said, probably stems from childhood learning experiences.

While I was able to agree with Bob on an intellectual level that what he said made sense and might even be true, it wasn't reaching me emotionally, down where I lived. My increased concentration at work was hard evidence that *something* was happening which now let me function 100 percent, even if it was for brief periods of time. The fact that I brought it up to Bob with the satisfaction of discovery indicated that something within me was celebrating a victory.

A Chameleon Identity

When I decided to seek some help from Bob, it was the first decision I had made in a long, long time. It seemed to be in my character not to decide things, especially if anyone else were involved. If my decision would affect or even come to the attention of another, I at once and without reservation sought the suggestions or advice of the other person.

An easy illustration has to do with eating. When I was on the road alone, I had no problem deciding what I wanted for dinner. But if anyone were with me, I would *invariably* wait until the other person had ordered and then almost always say, "Hey, that sounds good," and order what the other person had ordered. On those few times when I could not order second, I would order and then as soon as someone ordered something different I would say, "Hey, that sounds good," and change my order. Most of the time I thought I didn't really have a preference between the dishes. All of the time I thought the person or persons with me knew more than I did about restaurant food, so I would take my cue from them.

For a long time I would not buy any clothing without first getting Mary's opinion on the shirt or jacket or pants or even socks. "Do you like it?" I would ask. If she said she did, I would ask, "Should I buy it?" If she indicated I should, I would buy it. If she did not or gave no expression, I would not. More times than I like to think, Mary would try to get me to make a choice, but I would never do it. I couldn't make a choice. I just knew I didn't have any taste. I was sure I would choose the wrong color or cut.

It finally came down to what I would wear during the day. I would ask her what I should wear. On some days she simply wouldn't respond, in order to help me learn to make my own choices. Then I was uncomfortable all day long and often found fault with my choice of shirt, slacks, jacket, and tie.

During this time I knew I didn't feel as qualified as the next person to have an opinion on the subject at hand. Now, thinking back through it, I came to wonder about a couple of things.

> If someone else makes the decision, then I don't bear the responsibility if things go badly.
> If I don't take the responsibility, I never have to take the blame for anything.
> On the other hand, if things go well, I can enjoy the echoes of affirmation, having "joined" in the decision.

Bob pointed out that the right-brain/left-brain test had shown that the price I pay for this type of decision making is very high. That price is the frequent, almost constant anxiety I feel and the deep depression that sweeps over me periodically.

Another price I paid was that I didn't have an identity of my own. My identity changed the instant my environment changed. Bob had noted at the beginning of the session in which this was discussed that what I surround myself with, my setting, is of very great importance to me because I'm greatly affected by it. I take on and accommodate the "color" of the environment I find myself in.

That is why I was as careful as I could be about where I was and with whom I was associating. Possibly, it was also why I liked to be alone so much of the time. I had no identity of my own when I was not alone. I tended to think of myself as the classic introvert because of my desire to be alone. Therefore I could scarcely believe my ears when Bob told me I was a classic extrovert. In fact, here is the paragraph from my journal for that date.

Now, get this. Bob said I was a "classic extrovert." Imagine. He saw how startled I was because I have always thought of myself as just the opposite. But Bob said that an extrovert is one who is mightily aware of what is in his environment and reacts to it. An introvert is one who is not very sensitive to his environment and whatever is there doesn't matter all that much to him.

Bob stressed that my opinion on everything subjective is not a whit less valid than anyone else's opinion. No matter who likes something, if *I* don't like it, I don't like it. If I do like it and swallow my like, or deny it, I pay the price of not being myself.

But the fact is I was so entrenched in this manner of thinking I didn't know whether I liked something or not. Intellectually I could assent to Bob's idea, but on the level of my emotions, I felt he was wrong. I was not making decisions based on intellect but on emotions, so my assent did not mean much more than that I was allowing it as a possibility for future thinking.

Opposites Distract

It was amazing to me then and it is amazing to me still, but the guided discussion on my decision-making habits was in itself an intervention. It weakened the choke-hold that emotions had on my intellect. Within a few days I made this entry in the journal.

It is more than a tendency on my part to accept the opinions of others as being more valid than my own. Except in those areas in which I clearly excel—and there are few of them—I do within myself normally deem the expression of another to be the more authentic in the matter.

There are at least two possible components to this trait: (1) A distrust in the value of my own opinion. (2) A desire to avoid being held responsible for a mistake or bad call.

In looking at these two elements, I wonder if I could not determine that one is the nucleus of this atom and the other the element which whizzes around it, bound to conform by the structure of the atom but really secondary in primal cause.

Let's make the case both ways:

I was the only high schooler in a civic chorus conducted by a man whom I considered a good friend. He once said with a smile that if I was sight reading music and a note sounded wrong, I would know that I had either sung it wrong or that my ear was not attuned to what the arranger was accomplishing. And I agreed. It was a very long time later that it occurred to me that the arranger or score printer might have written a clinker.

The absence of self-confidence has been a dominant theme in all aspects of my life. The angst, the uncertainty, the concern, and the definitive feeling of incompetence were, and are to a lessening degree, there. I vividly recall in my earliest youth that I was neither the jack of all trades nor the master of any. How I wished then, as I actually do now, that I would be the master of at least one trade—anything.

So, the case can be made that because I feel so very incompetent in all things, I have sought the absence of responsibility as the best thing for the situation, and probably for me. If someone else chooses what I am to do or think, I will be better off than if *I* make that choice.

And that points up the second view of the case. The ultimate in freedom for a pinched soul is to be found not

responsible for a dumb decision. (That may account for
millions of footnotes in "scholarly" works!) That being so,
it is more than mere convenience that I would defer to the
judgment of others—it becomes essential.

Conclusion

I think we can draw this conclusion, that not having to
bear the responsibility is more central to the problem than
holding the opinion of others in higher esteem than my own
opinion.

In point of fact, a declared incompetence—averring that
you are a better judge on this kind of thing than I am—is a
ready alibi which may have no substance in truth. And it
surely has no substance in truth when the judgment to be
rendered is subjective, i.e., is red a better color than blue.

Going On

Let us say, then, that the desire for no or limited responsibility is *the* motivating factor. There still remains the question, *why* do I seek to limit my responsibility?

One reason suggested by the [results of the right-brain/
left-brain] test was the perfectionist trend in me. I don't like
to be associated with failure, and I hold a standard for myself that neither I nor anyone else could realize.

Before we go farther, if one of the rewards for this policy
is never having to say I'm sorry, one of the penalties which
make up the price of this habit is never to receive or accept
the fullness of credit for a thing accomplished. Another is
not to realize accomplishments which could be made if I
exercised my better judgment on a subject. These are very
high prices to pay.

Perfectionist tendencies are learned tendencies. They
come from outside us, from our environment. They come
from not living up to, or perceiving one's self as not living
up to, what one perceives as the reasonable expectations
of others.

I had a father whom I could not please. We had very little

contact, but my performance in those times did not please him. I did not live up to his expectations.

For instance, I didn't like peas as a very small child. (No right thinking very small child likes peas, but I didn't realize that at the time.) Here was an issue where I clearly failed him.

And I closed the journal for that day on what I now see was a poignant note:

My headaches as a child were extreme and debilitating. Maybe these were the results of my frustration in not being able to be the son Dad wanted. Or maybe they were my infantile way of reaching out, trying to open another avenue of communication. It didn't work. Mom rose to it. In fact, Mom loved it in one way because it made me more dependent upon her, but it didn't cut it with Dad.

A Significant Signal

One of the items in the right-brain/left-brain report warned that I "may be tempted to escape from [real life] into a substitute realm of experience formed of [my] own imagination." In reviewing this line, Bob and I recalled that I had in our first session mentioned that I had a lifelong fantasy that goes like this:

I come across a source of significant income which allows me to tell the person with whom I am in conflict, most often a person of authority in my life, that if he doesn't like what I tell him or what I do, he can lump it. If he likes it, I'll do it, otherwise I'm leaving because I no longer have to put up with his ideas.

Instead of finding that daydream a waste of time, Bob was excited about it. This, he said, was a really clear signal that there is a "me" in there. I have an identity that is crying to stand up and be heard. More than anything else in the world, it wants to get a chance to stand up and be counted. "This is extremely encouraging," he said.

Just a few weeks earlier I had begun to wonder if there was a real Deacon Anderson, and I wondered what he was like if there was one. Now Bob was saying there *is* a Deacon Anderson under that pile of problems that is smothering him. But *that* Deacon Anderson is buried under the one who compulsively yields to others, the one who doesn't seek to win but who seeks not to fail.

"We will begin small," Bob said. "We will practice determining opinions that are distinctively yours and avowing these opinions." It will take time. But we will do it.

DR. RICHARD:

In the early sessions two additional positive developments occurred for Deacon. First, he noted some increase in his ability to stay focused on a task. That is, his level and duration of concentration were improving. He began to realize that his difficulties in concentration were due largely to psychological factors and not neurological determinants. This meant, by implication, that concentration could be greatly improved as the psychological factors affecting it were resolved.

Second, and very important in the opening phases of therapy, Deacon came to see very clearly that he had a poorly developed sense of self. While he had a responsible job, *he frequently used relational strategies which helped him to avoid taking responsibilities.* Because he was always tuning in to other people's preferences in order to be the person whom he believed they would like (and thus gain their acceptance), he ended up not knowing what *he* really felt or liked. By not taking responsibility, he could never be wrong, but then *he could never have the satisfaction of being fully himself, right or wrong.*

Indeed, Deacon's daydreams revealed what he really wanted to feel and experience inside. *He wanted to be free to be the person he experienced himself to be in his dreams, which meant being confrontational and not having to please* everyone when that meant being true to his own feelings and opinions.

It is part of our essential destiny to be who God created us to be. We are not clones. We are unique individuals possessing unique combinations of gifts and abilities which may be used to enrich ourselves as well as others. God commands us to love our neighbors as ourselves. But loving and pleasing are not the same, though many persons confuse the two. Very slowly Deacon was beginning to see that to love does not always mean to please and that not having to always please means a new freedom to discover one's self in truth and honesty. Without this freedom we live a truncated life, a pitifully unfulfilled existence.

IV. THE HEALING

The difficult and painful journey toward wholeness

At the Lord's command,
Moses recorded the stages in their journey.
This is their journey by stages.

—Numbers 33:2, NIV

How long will your journey take?

—Nehemiah 2:6, NIV

ANDERSON:

The Healing Begins

As I have said, my dream life came alive when I got into therapy. It was then I became particularly aware of the value of dreams. In one of them, I had volunteered to accompany a very young Japanese boy as he symbolically ran into the Pacific Ocean on the last leg of a transcontinental marathon. There were no news people in attendance, just the boy and me.

We changed our running togs for bathing suits and then the boy dashed into the surf. I waited for him to turn and come back to shore, but he kept going until he was knocked over by a wave. This wasn't in the game plan. I plunged into the cold water and swam to where he was. By now he was heading back for shore, but the receding waves kept us exactly in place. Hard as we pumped, we could not get closer to the shore.

The boy tired and finally wrapped his small arms around my neck and held on. I was tired, too, and I began to worry that neither of us would make it back to shore, that we would both be swept out to sea and drown. But just as that concern became grave, I felt sand under my feet, and we swam to safety.

In analyzing this dream and others like it, Bob and I determined that such dreams alluded to trauma I experienced when I was a very small boy, probably between the ages of two and five. I always thought traumas were indelible incidents—the tattoos of life, which might fade or become blurry but always remained recognizable—but I had no explicit memories that I could identify as traumatic. Small wonder, really. If God gave me a good memory recorder, he forgot to supply the tape. Of course, it occurred to me that childhood trauma might be why I have little ability to remember things.

Clearly what I needed, we agreed, was not minor surgery to correct some surface problem. I needed the psychological equivalent of major surgery. First we would do exploratory work to find the abnormal growths that warped how I saw the world, and then we would proceed to reduce or remove those growths. This would be done at the cost of how I now perceived the world about me. I had to be prepared to match *reality* with how I *perceived reality*, and that can be a painful and traumatic experience.

Major surgery takes time, and so does the recovery process. Bob explained that therapy would demolish some of the very foundation blocks of my belief systems and that, he said, would be scary and painful. The time would be about a year—possibly more. My earlier right-brain/left-brain test and our conversations had indicated I had a good ability to link or make connections between ideas, and that is an aid to therapy.

I heard Bob out, and together we weighed the cost of making the commitment to go for the full treatment. In the ways already stated, I had no other choice. My journal entry for that day has some grisly overtones.

> I observed that I feel like I've been carrying around a dead child in me for fifty years and I want now either to mercifully inter him for all time or give him a chance, at last, to live. To decide to stay with counseling [as contrasted to therapy] would be to inter him, with no resultant satisfaction for the Deacon Anderson who remains.
>
> This is a significant turning point in my life, probably *the* turning point. Bob said I will be a discernibly different person when we are through. He said the process includes a period of time when I will become very dependent upon him and resent the fact that I am dependent. But he added that all of those who went through therapy and old pains found this to be a healing process, necessary to make them healthy.

It is interesting now, downstream of these observations, to note that Bob was not entirely correct in his assessment of my future estate (or in my perceptions of what he said), just as I was not entirely correct in my assessment of my estate. I *did* become a different person, but I never did resent the fact that I was dependent on Bob. In fact, my dependency was of a different sort than what I had expected. It was not onerous or burdensome. I generally looked forward to our sessions because I was strongly motivated to have a new understanding of life, and I worked hard at it.

To expedite the treatment, I asked if I could come in for sessions twice a week. Bob agreed we could try that schedule and back away from it if it became too tough. It *was* tough but we stuck with it for more than a year.

DR. RICHARD:

Now, shortly into the therapy process, Deacon faced another significant decision. He realized, as did I, that he needed major psychological "surgery." In order to receive the treatment required, he must now commit himself to the psychotherapy process, a commitment not wholly unlike a medical patient's committing himself or herself to a serious surgical procedure.

I make a distinction between *counseling* and *psychotherapy*. Both processes bring about change but at different levels of complexity and consciousness. *Counseling* typically is focused on problem-solving. It is designed to help the individual approach personal and relational problems on a primarily rational, conscious basis. Most counseling approaches assume the client does not possess any severely limiting thinking disorders (e.g., paranoia, reasoning difficulties, or mental distortions associated with alcohol or other drug use) and is reasonably stable emotionally (not subject to deep depressions or intense levels of anxiety). Dealing with marital problems, job-related difficulties, or conflicts with important persons such as one's children, parents, or in-laws are examples of when the counseling process is appropriate. Counseling is relatively short-term, lasting anywhere from two to six months and occasionally longer, with a successful outcome seeing the problems either resolved or greatly ameliorated. While there will be some changes within the client in terms of behavior and attitudes, these changes are not nearly as profound as those which occur in psychotherapy.

The *psychotherapy* process is designed to address the conscious as well as unconscious aspects of the human mind, and brings about complex internal changes which affect one's perception of the self, others, the world, and even God. It is a much longer process, usually requiring a year or more of regular sessions, most often once a week. Psychotherapy is not appropriate or even desirable for everyone. While all of us could benefit from a heightened understanding of ourselves and a healing of old emotional wounds, psychotherapy seems to be especially meaningful to those who have had an emotionally debilitating childhood and/or adolescence and who come into adulthood with a set of perceptions, behaviors, and emotions that continually burden them inwardly and contribute importantly to poor and unfulfilling interpersonal relationships. However, it should be emphasized that persons in need of psychotherapy are *not crazy* in the sense that they function at a minimal level in life. Many, like Deacon, are quite functional but are deeply distressed and unless the distress is dealt with and relieved, they may become dysfunctional.

Deacon's decision for psychotherapy was indeed probably *the* turning point in his adult life. Deacon needed more than the minor surgery of counseling. He needed the major surgery of psychotherapy, and we both knew it with certainty after a few sessions.

ANDERSON:

Alone

As if I hadn't enough problems, a new one piled on top of all of the others. Therapy made me feel adrift in a hostile environment, and more than before, I was all alone. It was not the loneliness of not knowing anyone on a crowded bus. It was a far more terrifying loneliness that comes when one methodically abandons everything he knows to be true. The firm, if painful, ground I knew and hated but trusted now turned into quicksand.

I presumed my problem was that the world as I experienced it was a paint-by-number world and that I had used red where I should have used green. But it wasn't that way at all. I found I didn't even know where the lines were. I was entirely lost. Once I began to question my perceptions, nothing made very much sense.

I recalled a short story I had read in *The New Yorker* many years earlier. In it a gangster mob had gotten revenge on a rival mob leader by kidnapping his son. They beat him so terribly that he was left a quadriplegic, without sight, hearing, or physical sensation. Unable to communicate or receive information, the young man began to live a fantasy life in his mind, a life where he was alive and well. He peopled his imagination with a whole society, including a beautiful girl to whom he became engaged. On his wedding day, his radiant bride beside him, he was ready to take the vows when he became aware of a disturbance in the church. As from a very great distance, he heard a voice: "Don't worry, son. We're going to pull you through. You're coming back." Although it had been impossible to restore his sight, the use of his limbs, or his sense of touch, a medical team had done radical surgery to restore his hearing—and in doing so had ruined the only hope the young man had for any kind of happiness.

As I remembered that story, I wondered if I had now ruined the only hope I had for happiness. I was alone in a more profound sense than the young man in the story, for I had not peopled my mind with a substitute society.

Reflecting on this story and on some of my dreams, I noted in the journal:

This may reflect my concern about yesterday's session. I'm really alone on this venture. No one can go with me. No one can understand my current circumstances, why what appears so simple to others seems so hard to me. I alone know that that is true. I'm not sure where I'm going. I'm only sure I want to get out of where I am.

DR. RICHARD:

As psychotherapy progresses, a sense of leaving what-has-been for what-will-evolve begins to occur. This, for most people, is a scary ordeal and always involves facing festering emotional pain. In its opening stages, psychotherapy often is not a pleasant process. No wonder that some people do not carry out the process to its conclusion or else never begin, choosing to live with their present misery in preference to risking a commitment to the unknown pain of psychotherapy.

The sense of aloneness which Deacon experienced is not unusual. It was generated by questioning many of his cherished notions about himself, the world, and his place in it. But what Deacon realized—and what others in the psychotherapy process also experience—is that the aloneness has a quality about it which we come to know when we truly confront ourselves deeply and personally. That is, there are places of the mind where only we can go—*no one can really go with us,* except God, and he is always there even though we may not always sense his presence. It is this feeling of aloneness, not unlike that which may be experienced in the process of dying, which so many find frightening and repeatedly attempt to avoid—often at the great price of never obtaining life-changing self-knowledge or understanding.

ANDERSON:

A Time to Cry

At some point not noted in my journal, I learned how to cry. It happened as I was telling Bob how terribly disturbed I became when I saw a parent abusing his or her child, as occasionally happens in a public place. It is all I can do to restrain myself from intervening on behalf of the child, but I know that if I do, I will do something terrible to the parent.

Everyone hates to see a child abused, but the quality of my hate was something overwhelming. I would have to leave the scene immediately, before I blew up. Concern for the child's welfare would linger in my mind for several hours.

Even before Bob and I got into the discussion, I began to break up. I am not a crier. Crying was against all I stood for. Yet as I tried to explain what happened inside me when I saw unfair treatment of a child, I could speak only in short, painful bursts between bouts of crying. At first, I fought to contain the crying—but once the tears had begun to flow, I fought to go ahead and cry. The go-ahead won, and I cried as a child in unspeakable pain. It felt good to really cry.

My father held crying in contempt, and I learned early on not to cry . . . almost ever. That worked to my advantage as a reporter and editor. I was rarely emotionally distressed by even the most dire circumstance. Facts were facts. We live in an unfair world and have to deal with the world as we find it. The chink in my armor was when children were involved. The untimely death of a youngster affected me, particularly if the youngster had met a violent death.

But I didn't cry.

In a very narrow range of circumstances, I would very nearly weep—for instance, at a parade. As the marching units approached, I would get a strange, unaccountable lump in my throat and my eyes would well with tears. As best as I can describe it, my feeling was that what was happening was "so good, so right." The same feeling would sweep through me when I saw a happy family or when I enjoyed a concert. It was such a beautiful experience of "togetherness." Yet at the same time, I was possessed of a terrible sadness.

Was I almost crying out of joy, or out of sorrow? If joy, why was I sad? If sorrow, why sorrow in the middle of something so enjoyable? Why did I not feel like crying when any normal person would weep, when the circumstances obviously warranted tears?

The answers to those questions did not surface in the early sessions. I hurt too badly to do much thinking about it.

DR. RICHARD:

In the psychotherapy process, Deacon soon encountered an emotional block that he was able to face and move through. This was a further encouraging step. Consciously, Deacon could recall his father discouraging crying. He had some idea of why it was hard to let the tears flow. But he only dimly understood how certain circumstances elicited a strong urge to cry. This is another excellent example of what persons experience when there is "live" emotional pain from years past. A specific setting or scene taps into the unconscious, and unexpected emotions rise to the surface. Only now Deacon was beginning to give himself permission to both *feel and express* the emotions. The events which triggered Deacon's desire to cry were further indications of considerable unconscious pain associated with his childhood. That there was a connection to the past was readily apparent when he observed that his crying was not in response to circumstances that "obviously warranted tears." The emotional responses were a poor "fit" to current experience.

ANDERSON:

Mary

There were three things going for me as I began to deal with my perceptions of the world and of myself. There was God, whom I understood loved me without my knowing why. There was Mary, my wife of thirty years. Prior to my entering therapy, Mary had come to psychological terms with a passionless past. And there was Bob, my psychotherapist. Take away any of those three, and I would likely have continued in my death spiral.

For instance, had I not been able to "play back" my therapy sessions with Mary, I don't think I could have processed some of the emotional storms that besieged me. She was always there, always listening, ever wise, never playing the therapist but always being an interested listener and encourager.

Mary's lucid insights served as a kind of buffer between where I had been and where I was heading. The real world had not unfolded yet, but it was about to. Her confidence, her empathy, her understanding were solid and assuring.

She witnessed to her own progress. Raised in what can only be called primitive social, psychological, and academic environments with *no* parental support, married to a man she didn't understand very well and who did not understand her, she had not long before determined to get unstuck from her early life. She sought the help she needed, received it, and came out of her parentally-defined box into the real world.

Now she was a bit like a live-in lay counselor who never overstepped her knowledge or authority but who never backed away from what she could do, either. Mary, like Bob and God, was critical to my survival.

Bob

In a way, this whole book is about what Bob did in my life. He became deeply, unreservedly involved with me without becoming responsible for me. He felt what I felt without becoming a part of the problem so that he could remain a part of the solution. He was a wise and skilled guide who sensed when to plunge ahead and when to ease off, when to encourage and when to cool down.

In one sense he was restoring a human vehicle that had been in a terrible wreck and was headed for the junkyard, so that a person who had never had a chance to grow could now have that chance. In another sense he was holding last rites for a person who should never have been born, dismantling the unsound person once and for all.

He did what time and environment could not do, or rather, he undid what time and environment had done. It is beyond the shadow of a doubt that I was in a death spiral when I came to Bob. I believed I was quite literally dying.

So in part this book is public acknowledgment of Bob's work in my life and a confirmation to evangelical Christians that skilled and sensitive evangelical psychologists are of inestimable value in helping people find healing.

God

And in part this book is public acknowledgment of God's work in my life. For me, an evangelical Christian, the bedrock of my life is not of this world but of eternity. There *is* a God who has shown himself in the empirical universe in the person of Jesus Christ. It is this God, this underlying presence whom I know, who was and is the indivisible truth. Here at least and at last was Truth. *This I knew.* All else was, to me, theory and subject to doubt. As the world swirled about me, there was always this: I knew him and was known by him. Thus, while I knew I was lost, I knew also that I was not forsaken.

Not all of these things were in my mind when, early in therapy, I dreamed the following:

> I was driven in a cab to a garage where I was told to find my skis. The skis were stacked five feet high and there were thousands of them.
>
> I had no idea where my skis were. In fact, I had never had a pair of skis in my life and didn't know for certain there were any skis here assigned to me.

After stewing about a bit, I was upset with the cab driver because I thought he was supposed to help me find my skis. I bent down to the first level of skis and looked at the lowest set of skis and found these were mine. I pulled them out, double checked them against a heretofore mysterious list of identifying numbers I kept in my billfold. They were mine. I was on my way to notify the cab driver when I woke up.

I think Bob was the cab driver who has been sitting in the driver's seat of the cab, but we haven't really gone anywhere. I feel I'm looking without help for meaning, and the job is overwhelming. In that I found my skis, I think that represents hope that I will be able to go on without the cab later on.

Discontent with the direction of therapy surfaced more frequently than I may have mentioned to Bob. But underneath it all was the knowledge that this was the *only* way for me to go and that I would not quit the going.

DR. RICHARD:

One's network of supportive relationships plays a vital role in the process of change that takes place during therapy. By supportive relationships I mean those relationships with family and friends where we can basically "be ourselves" and feel accepted and valued for who we are and not for the roles we play. Such relationships are usually focused on what is best for us and help provide a favorable emotional climate for change. Some persons have an extensive and active support network. For others, the network is very limited, with only one or two relationships which may be considered truly supportive.

Deacon's support network, humanly speaking, was minimal, as it often is with persons who have not developed well psychologically. However, his wife Mary was a key support person. Not only did she provide steadfast encouragement and sensitive listening, she also had become a model for personal growth. Deacon had observed *her* changes, and this in turn was additional incentive for his own.

In a real sense, the psychotherapist also becomes part of the client's support network. When the client's support network is limited, the therapist may play an even more influential role. I realized that, during the course of treatment, Deacon would become dependent on me in several ways. He would be looking toward me to provide direction, stimulate insights, and design interventions which would facilitate change leading to growth out of his painful existence.

The key phrase which Deacon used to describe our relationship, and which can characterize any good therapist/client relationship, was that *I became deeply, unreservedly involved with him without becoming responsible for him.* Encompassed within this statement is the recognition of deep caring on the therapist's part, yet there is also the realization that the client's decisions are ultimately his or her responsibility and not the therapist's. Thus, as a therapist I am responsible *to* but not *for* my clients. Psychotherapy, then, is a partnership. It is a relationship two persons enter, each agreeing to carry out their respective tasks. The therapist uses his skills to assist the client in developing new awareness, finding healing, instigating change in behavior; but it is only the client who can be open to new awareness and who can actually instigate change. Without the client assuming full responsibility for his or her life, the psychotherapy process is doomed, just as it is doomed when the therapist tries to usurp the responsibility that rightfully belongs to the client.

God had always been an integral part of Deacon's life, and even through his struggles and doubts, Deacon had maintained his faith. God was an immutable reference point for Truth and gave him a sense of security in an otherwise painful, dreary, and confusing personal world. While Deacon could not connect exactly how his problems could be related to or not related to God's work in his life, he never felt forsaken. His faith became a genuine means for providing psychological support. Thus his relationship with God must be understood as a real part of his support network.

Deacon is one of many persons whose faith can be a sustaining source of hope and encouragement in times of crisis and change. It is important to point out here that when a Christian client works with a Christian therapist, there is an implicit (and sometimes explicit) agreement on the basic nature and purpose of the universe and mankind's existence on earth. While these cosmic issues may have little to do directly with a client's specific problem, both the client and therapist know they are working within the same framework and thus share many of the same values and perspectives in regard to a variety of ethical and moral questions. Research into the results of psychotherapy strongly suggest that the more similar client and therapist values are, the more likely it is there will be a positive psychotherapeutic outcome.

Deacon's dream about the cab driver reflects what many people feel in the early stages of therapy—a lack of certainty about direction and nagging questions about what the whole process will really produce. I often remind my clients to see psychotherapy for what it is—a *process* which takes time and which, because it is so complex, must proceed in stages. A large mountain is not climbed in a day. It is climbed through the establishment of a series of camps. And it is this progression which eventually allows the climber to make the final assault to the top. To think about climbing a high mountain seems impossible unless the climb can be visualized as occurring in several stages. So it is with psychotherapy. It is a process which goes through stages leading to an ultimate goal. To see the goal without visualizing the steps leading to it can be, as with the mountain, overwhelming.

ANDERSON:

Dad

As we got into the third month of therapy, we took up my perceptions of the relationships in my life. These sessions primarily centered on memories of my relationship with my dad. Only one thing was wrong. I didn't remember very much about him. The following journal entry notes this:

> Bob said the "blocking" I experience does not indicate the absence of memory but the encasing of painful memory.
>
> A child learns by emotional experience for the first six or so years of his life, and *then* he begins to intellectualize about his experiences with the emotional background already in place.
>
> I intellectually accept and agree with our conclusions, but it doesn't seem to make any difference. This may be because the imprint of my emotional experience predated my intellectual experience.
>
> I was programmed to avoid failure, but a cousin of that program is the program to avoid success. To achieve success would be to find myself a worthy person, and I know I'm not a worthy person. To succeed would bring me all kinds of complications.

It was necessary for us to bring to awareness my relationship with Dad in my tender years before I could come to grips with the way I perceived the world about me today.

Dad was a workaholic, very tough, a really good administrator. He was an evangelical minister with what I think must have been modest preaching abilities. He was not very much of a people person, as far as I could tell. (I bear in mind the limited exposure a minister's child may have to his father.) Dad probably went to his grave without ever once thinking about the tiered relationships in his life. By tiered I mean his order of priorities was 1—God, 2—church, 3—

family, 4—anything else, and I'm not sure the last two are in the right order.

Dad's priority in life was to serve the Lord, only. That was the extent of his commitment. It seems odd to reflect that I cannot recall Dad's ever hugging or kissing me. He may have, but I don't think he did. He was not a hugger or kisser. I can only once recall seeing him kiss Mom, and that was when he was leaving for somewhere and a lot of people were about. He was embarrassed into giving her a peck on the cheek. I never saw him hug her, that I can recall. They never held hands. Never touched.

Dad preached frequently on the love of God, but he always frowned as he spoke. I can't remember what he said about the love of God, but I can still see the frown. His messages about God's love always left me feeling like an ingrate. In fact, my dominant recollection of our relationship is the way he looked at me, his dark eyes always flashing with what I took to be molten hate. I don't remember ever seeing love in his eyes. His least threatening look was suspicion and intimidation, freighted with unspoken messages of disapproval or outright disgust.

Insofar as I can remember, I never in my entire young life did anything that Dad approved of. I don't recall his ever encouraging me in anything, although he may have. He seemed simply not to approve of me as a human being. I could not succeed with him. He took no pride in me. When he considered me at all, it was as an embarrassment or a disappointment.

Although I could not think of a specific occasion, nevertheless I had imbedded in my mind the notion that Dad must have punished me with some regularity. I had to turn to others for any data on punishment. My sister told me about the time I slipped a book in my pants over the target area to cut down on the pain of a spanking. She said Dad's first swat was so hard it injured his hand or wrist so badly he could not continue the punishment. I was no more than six at the time.

Even to this day I cannot recollect much physical punishment, although I do remember hard pain when he doubled his fist and hit me behind the ear for not doing some homework. I saw it for what it was, a lashing out in anger rather than a deserved correction meted out.

Even with skimpy evidence, I am certain the punishment he meted out was inevitably severe, that it never fit the crime, that in his eyes there was no such thing as petty wrongdoing, only mortal wrongdoing. I feel that *no matter what I did,* good or bad, the very doing of it caused me to become a candidate for punishment.

Bob described Dad's attitude as rejection, and on an intellectual level, I agreed with him. But I didn't need to intellectualize to see myself as a zip, a nothing, a nonentity, a nuisance just by being alive. I accepted as valid Dad's treatment of me.

As a child, I was unable to assimilate that Dad's rejection was unwarranted. I saw myself as the legitimate cause of his rejection. Even when I knew it wasn't of my doing, I *felt* it was of my doing. After all, Dad was Dad, *the* authority figure for all of life, the shepherd of the flock, the man of God.

During this session I remembered that as a very small child, I had whooping cough, which at the time was often a fatal ailment. I remember feeling tremendous guilt because I was sick. I was again a disappointment to Dad.

At the end of the session, Bob shook his head and said it was a wonder I had survived at all, and really amazing that I had done as well professionally and personally as I had done. Well, maybe he's right.

Mom was the reason I survived.

Mom

My formative years were lived in constant fear and terror, which was manifested in conformity to all the rules, written and unwritten. I had a creative thought life but never dared to give expression to it. My low self-esteem was matched in part by an active, if not necessarily wholesome, thought life. With no vent for expression, I likely would not have survived childhood without Mom. Mom's nurturing made my early life tolerable.

In many ways, Mom was the opposite of Dad. Mom was not a strong woman. Dad would never have married a strong woman. Almost certainly he was intimidated by them, so he married his shy farm-girl sweetheart after an eight-year engagement while he finished his education. Mom made up for a tenderness which Dad could not give me.

The hugs and kisses and back rubs and words of encouragement and praise made early life tolerable. Bob believed I would have grown up to be a completely different person had I not had Mom's nurturing and thus managed to survive childhood more or less intact.

Mom loved me, but she feared Dad more than she loved me and never once, to my recollection, intervened on my behalf or on the behalf of fairness and justice when Dad meted out punishment. Never once, in all those years do I recall her speaking up in my behalf. That lesson took deep root. Here the one I loved freely and openly above all others did not find me worthy of defending before an oppressive father, even when both of us *knew* I was in the right. "You know Dad," she would sometimes say. I realize now she was intimidated by most things in life, and utterly terrified of Dad.

DR. RICHARD:

At our seventh session, I began to find out what Deacon could consciously remember about his history. Beginning then, and for several subsequent sessions, we looked at his childhood, adolescence, young and mature adulthood.

Getting a good personal history is invaluable for both the therapist and the client. It allows the therapist to get a sense of the significant relationships, events, and patterns that have helped shape the client's life. Furthermore, the client often begins to see how early experiences are connected with present distorted perceptions and troublesome attitudes and behaviors. In short, getting a good history is an essential learning experience and foundational to the therapy process.

The most significant and influential people in our early lives are our parents, or parent surrogates. It was clear that Deacon's father played a dominant role in his childhood and adolescent years. As Deacon verbalized what he could remember about childhood years with his father, it became obvious that his relationship with this parent was seriously disturbed, and that his father did not provide the kind of psychological and spiritual nourishment which must be present to help new human beings grow up and become healthy adults. Because of his father's behavior, the seeds of Deacon's self-doubt and self-hate were sown very early. As a child, Deacon did something we *all* do in regard to our parents. We judge our parents' reactions toward us and evaluations of us as normative, as valid, since as children we have no other standard by which to measure ourselves. If we feel we are falling short of a parent's desires, if we feel rejected by a parent, if a parent displaces anger on us inappropriately, we inevitably feel there is something *wrong* with us, otherwise our parent would not be reacting as he or she does. A child simply is unable to perceive that the parent's reactions may result from his or her own emotional disturbances.

It is only later, after damage has already been done, that the child may begin to realize that the parent is not next to God in knowledge and power, that he or she is a *human being* with strengths and weaknesses unique to his or her personality. This later realization, at a significant inner emotional level, represents a *major step forward* in the maturing process of any individual, for it allows the child to begin to view reality about himself or herself through his or her *own* eyes and no longer through the eyes of the parent. As this process begins to occur, a whole new set of self-perceptions begin to emerge, and the journey toward healing the early damage has begun.

Often, and fortunately for the child, where one parent is significantly deficient, the other fills in the gaps by giving what the one parent lacks. Deacon's mother was the nurturer in his family and supplied the emotional support, acceptance, and warmth which his father was sorely unable to supply. Had Deacon not received this nurturing, it is likely that his sense of self-worth would have been even lower, and he likely would have suffered a more serious and debilitating emotional disorder.

Though his mother did give the missing support, her fear of her husband was stronger than her love for Deacon. Thus she consistently allowed emotional and even some physical abuse to be carried out by her husband toward her child.

It became obvious to me that Deacon grew up in a setting which exhibited patterns classically associated with abusive families. Usually the weaker parent in the marital relationship will silently and passively consent to the abuse by the other parent, often out of fear (sometimes justified, sometimes not) that something terrible will happen should the abusive spouse be stoutly confronted. It is a sad fact of life that far too many marital relationships are based on the fear one spouse has of the other, causing them to become locked into behaviors that are destructive both to themselves and their children.

When one spouse goes along with the abusive behavior of the other, the message given to the child is exactly the one Deacon received—the child is not worthy of defending. How many adults have sat in my office and vented their anger, sorrow, and frustration over a parent who could have assisted them in their childhood helplessness, but did not! Such actions only serve to further confirm the child's developing sense of worthlessness and powerlessness.

ANDERSON:

Selfishness and Self-Love

There is a flip side to the subject of nourishment, and it is deprivation. I had learned as a small child that I was not worthy of emotional nourishment. Any nourishment I got, such as that from my mom, I took as unexpected and unde-served. I did little to seek nourishment myself.

In fact, Bob told me one day that I probably had never nourished myself emotionally. To enjoy myself was wrong. I was not one worthy of enjoying. During our conversation I told him I was at times powerfully moved by shapes, forms, lines, sounds, shadows, color, and textures. I had told him about a car I admired, a car which favorably exhibited several of these elements. Bob suggested that what I liked about the car fell directly in line with nourishing myself emotionally.

I must have believed him. The next Saturday I bought the big car. I flew in the face of my feelings about myself, the guilt associations, the inner protests of unworthiness, and bought the car. It was a bold psychological step for me and one loaded with emotional risks, but it turned out to be a significant symbol of faith in better days to come.

Bob and I noted that before the Fall, Adam certainly loved himself as God's creation. He did not *worship* himself nor love himself in excess of his love for God. But he knew him-self, accepted himself, appreciated himself as God's handi-work, and felt comfortable in God's love, and thus in his own.

DR. RICHARD:

Because Deacon felt so undesirable as a child, it became very difficult for him to value himself. A direct outcome of not valuing one's self is the failure to do those things which are good for or that nurture the self. *Thus Deacon missed seeing and doing the very things that would help him the most.* He simply did not know how to take care of himself in a loving way, because any healthy sense of self-love was nonexistent.

We come now to an area that has often been seriously misunderstood by many Christians—the relationship between self-love on the one hand and self-centeredness on the other. I grew up hearing the slogan "love God first, others second, and yourself last." Based on a more biblical theology and recent psychological research, as well as personal experience, I no longer believe the slogan to be accurate. In fact, teaching based on that slogan has helped to perpetuate low self-esteem in many Christians and has ended up actually hampering and damaging their relationships with others.

In the beginning God created mankind, and it was good. We all know that sin entered the world, and the account given in Genesis 3 shows that the man and woman acted on their own apart from God's explicit command, thus setting their own judgment above that of God. Such action may be said to be the essence of self-centeredness and pride. But it is not grounds for self-hate, nor does it negate the need for self-love.

Throughout the Bible God's love for his people, in spite of their sin, is the central thread of redemption. It is in this context that Jesus calls us to love our neighbor as we love ourselves (Matt. 22:34-40). Paul points out a direct relationship between loving one's self and loving one's spouse (Eph. 5:28-29). The implication is, of course, that if one does not love one's self, it is extraordinarily difficult, if not impossible, to *maturely* love someone else. I emphasize *maturely* because the person with little self-love may *appear* to love others; however, it is not genuine love, but an attachment driven by a strong need for approval, validation, dependency, or control. *It is not a caring, supportive, and nurturing love.* Others sense this and thus often pull away from such pseudo-love, much to the confusion of the person who exhibits it.

What are some of the attributes of healthy self-love? *Genuine self-love has its basis in God's love for us.* God, through Jesus Christ, provides us with the model for loving ourselves. The challenge for us (and it can be a *great* challenge if we have been psychologically damaged) is to implement it in our lives. What is the essence of this model of God's love? Just this: It involves *forgiveness* (letting go and moving on), *acceptance* (starting with who I am and progressing toward who I want to become), *affirmation* (being redeemed and feeling good about myself), *nurturing* (doing kindly, helpful things for myself so that I may grow), and *confrontation* (not denying, avoiding, and running away, but confronting reality as it is).

As our self-love begins to exhibit these characteristics, we will find ourselves not only liking ourselves much more, but we will find it much easier to have mature and loving relationships with others, since we have the capacity now to extend to them the very kind of love we extend to ourselves.

Interestingly, and importantly, psychological studies in the area of self-esteem consistently find that people who like themselves and have high self-regard are rated by others as being loving and caring individuals. Thus, both from theological and psychological viewpoints, self-love forms the basis for truly loving relationships.

But what about self-centeredness? Self-centeredness is really qualitatively different from self-love. In self-centeredness we witness an *excessive* focus on one's own needs and desires to the exclusion of others' concerns. Self-centeredness is fundamentally self-protective and defensive, and the person consumed with it is unable to love others with any degree of maturity. Usually deep feelings of personal insecurity and inadequacy underlie self-centeredness. Thus self-focused behavior becomes a way of trying to cope with these internal difficulties. The truly self-centered person drives others away and may end up feeling isolated. By his behavior, such a person ends up creating the very alienation he or she does not want and then usually ends up blaming others for the resulting break-downs in relationships.

To me, there is no question that persons whose childhood has severely damaged their ability to develop healthy self-love need psychological treatment. It is virtually impossible to get through the pain, find the healing, and maintain growth without assistance. From the Christian therapist's perspective, this is precisely the point at which God can use another human being and his or her skills to help bring about the healing and change which makes true self-love possible.

What about the slogan I mentioned earlier? Some rearrangement is necessary: It is still God first, but then it is you second and others third. Without a priority on love for yourself, there never will be a true ability to love others.

ANDERSON:

Safety in Unaccountability

At this stage in my therapy, the fear of failure was overwhelming, just as it had been all through my life. I would do almost *anything* to avoid becoming accountable because I didn't want to risk failing. Failure was my true identity, but I had to, by any means available, keep that my secret. *I was a failure.* It wasn't that I was someone who failed once or who failed frequently. I *was* a failure.

Bob confronted me head-on. "This is unreal," he said. "The dire consequences of the failure you mortally dread don't exist. *Everyone* fails. Failing does not have the consequences you perceive it to have."

"I hear what you're saying," I said, "but I'm incapable of *feeling* what you are saying."

"I know you are," he said back. "That's one of the reasons you're here."

"Knowing something intellectually and accepting it emotionally are two different things," I said, "and even my dreams plainly show that I'm not sure my way of thinking is subject to change."

"It *is* subject to change," Bob insisted, "and do you know why? Motivation to change is 90 percent of the battle, and you're about as highly motivated as a person can be."

It struck me that he was as certain of his position as I was uncertain of mine. Bob's job now was to try to find a common ground, one where I would be reasonably comfortable.

"If we cannot completely eradicate that fear, we can sure ameliorate it in the future," he said with singular confidence. I listened. He said that one of the tools he would use was regression therapy, which might open up past experiences so I can reprocess them.

Instead of being pleased with this pronouncement, I was scared by it.

Preparing to Regress

I didn't tell Bob that the idea of regression frightened me in a couple of ways. A dream I had suggests one of those ways.

> I was in a building and in a hurry to get outside. In seeking an exit, I found myself to be near the loading-dock door. I rushed to the door to pull it open and leave, only to find it locked.
>
> I turned to find something to pry the door open, and I noticed that a Chinese fellow carrying keys was entering the room. He smiled and nodded and headed for the door. I waited impatiently as he fumbled about finding the right key.
>
> While this was happening, I came to understand that something had changed; if I inhaled in this room, I would inhale water, and I would drown. I realized I didn't have enough breath within me to last until the door had opened.

I dashed for a small office about thirty feet away. A man was reading in the office. I got in, closed the door and wondered if I was now going to drown when I inhaled. But I had to breathe, so I did.

It was air I was breathing, not water. I filled my lungs to capacity, then saw that the loading-dock door to the outside was now open, and ran through the dock to safety outside.

This dream suggested to me that I was drowning in my fears and that the routine elements of life were not going to save my life. The room with the man sitting in it was probably the therapy experience with Bob. I could breathe in here, breathe enough to make it to safety. I had to go through the waters of regression to make it, but I *could* make it.

That was one of the reasons I feared regression. I thought it might kill me. I can't explain why I thought this, but it was a very real fear at the time.

Another clue to my fear of the regression therapy is found in another brief dream recorded in my journal:

On Saturday night I dreamed that a group of us were putting together a television game show. I recall none of the details, but I do recall that the title was "Getting Rid of People."

This suggests that, after my discussion with Bob on Saturday morning and a later discussion I had with Mary about perhaps recalling in subsequent sessions specific bad memories, my mind is wrestling with the idea of letting loose some of the memory images I have of some people and letting other images take their places.

Maybe "dissembling" is in part the process of remembering what actually happened, instead of what I think had happened.

At the moment I have little hope for my capacity to regress. My chief concern may be that I am convinced my defense mechanisms will utterly prevent me from regressing.

Other dreams were confrontational. In one of my dream interpretations, I noted that "part of me is saying, 'Don't go

out there and wrestle with the issues. They'll slice you up.'
The other part of me is saying, 'Go ahead. Gut it out and
everything will turn out better than it is right now.'"

The Whale, the Bear, and the Elephant

For me, one of the more formidable challenges in writing
this narrative has been to help the reader make sense of the
way I *used* dreams to understand where I was in the therapy
process. Dreams became my psychological dipstick. Bob
and I found them to be saturated with meaning, a rich
source of new information almost every night.

Dreams do not forecast where you are going. But they do
pinpoint your location within the framework of all you are
experiencing at the time. Dreams show the frontier of your
emotional life. Bearing in mind that your emotional life
shapes your intellectual life, it is worth the effort to assess
your location, particularly in times of stress. Once you know
where you are, you are in a better position to determine
which direction to take from that point.

Here are two dreams that helped me understand my position, what I thought of myself, as I was approaching the
regression sessions.

Mary and I were in an odd tourist attraction in a desert.
The attraction featured a giant bear and a huge whale.

I thought I would be most interested in the whale, but the
bear interested me much more. The bear was huge. He must
have been twelve feet tall. When we first saw him, he was
standing on his hind legs facing a wall and seemed to be
pulling mindlessly on the wire screen which covered a window to the outside. We watched for a short time, then went
to see the whale.

The whale was kept in a tubular tank which was like a
very large pipe cut in two lengthwise. The sorry creature
was only a little bit shorter than the tub and could not move
at all. In fact, I wasn't sure if it was alive or dead.

Two stupid tourists, thin men in their sixties, found a way
close to the whale's head, and there they jumped up and

down like vaudeville clowns, and then left. I presumed they were trying to scare him or show their dominance over this enormous mammal. I was very upset with their actions and thought them insulting to the whale.

We returned to the first exhibit to find the bear now wearing old, blue overalls and looking really silly, like a Disney character. Two other old and thin men were in the bear's area and were talking with him in a patronizing way, making fun of him, and he was talking with them.

I understood that the bear was intelligent, even very intelligent, and that if he decided to use his intelligence and great strength, he could take these guys apart in a moment. He turned toward them and they backed up nervously and threw some green hay toward the bear to confuse him. I don't know if he was confused or not, but he stopped heading toward them.

As Mary and I left the exhibition, I said to the bear, "Why don't you take off those stupid overalls and be yourself?" Whether or not I said it, I don't know, but I was thinking that the bear had more intelligence than any of the men we had seen, and that intelligence had to be reckoned with. I realized that the bear had the mental resources to fight his circumstances in a court of law and to win freedom from the cage and the respect of those about him.

As I considered this dream, I thought both the whale and the bear represented me. The whale was the dying-if-not-dead hulk of the old me, the one who had lived and struggled for so many years, only to find himself helpless in the face of harassment by unthinking people. The whale, the old me, was a goner. Let him be in peace.

The bear, on the other hand, was becoming discontent with his lot in life. He wanted out of the window. He was dangerous and a genuine threat to those who harassed him, and he was preparing to quit pretending he was like those who dressed him in their kind of clothes. He was himself, and he would be himself.

My journal notes following the dream said:

I don't have to pretend to be somebody. I *am* somebody, and I ought to come out and just be myself. I've got the wherewithal to do it.

The next night I had a similar dream.

I shared the responsibility of feeding two elephants and, on this occasion, was going to give them a special treat of oats which I carried in a bag. The barn door seemed to be stuck as I tried to enter it, and I saw an elephant's enormous leg against the inside of the door. I pushed the door hard and the leg moved, but the animal didn't get up. I squeezed through the door and found the elephant to be very old, with shiny and flaccid legs and trunk. My friend was in front of the elephant and poured some of the oats in a trough. The animal began to pick the oats up with his trunk.

I took my bag and climbed a ramp that overlooked the area of the second elephant, a slightly smaller and very rambunctious animal. As I got near to him, he charged me. I shouted that I had food, and he settled down. I threw him a handful of oats and he began to eat. I looked into the bag to get another load of oats, and when I looked up, the elephant was not there. Instead I found small, mean-looking wart hogs dashing about where the elephant had been.

I looked in the direction of the door and saw the elephant there kind of rampaging, very nervous and bothered about something. He wanted the oats, and no wart hogs were a threat to him. I ran over to him, scared to death but knowing the animal wasn't angry with me. Then I saw he was wearing a seamless black plastic coat or film which entirely encompassed his back and belly. It was airtight, and it was obviously what was bothering him. He could not get a grasp on it to throw it off.

I said something to the effect that I hoped he understood. Then I grabbed the slick cloth and swung right under the elephant and took out my pen knife. I hoped I didn't accidentally stab the elephant as I made a cut into the film. It split away as I cut it and soon the entire sheet simply sloughed off the animal.

He instantly calmed down. His spirits rose, and he headed back as happy as could be to where I had tossed the oats.

There were several very important things in this dream. I *shared the responsibility* of the feeding. I think Bob was the person with whom this responsibility was shared.

The door was jammed. I could get in only after *exerting real effort*. It was jammed by the leg of the dying elephant, the old me. The person with whom I shared the feeding responsibilities, Bob, fed the old elephant, but it remained old and dying.

I went on to the other animal who was itching to get going. He was frisky and animated, but he was suffocating, in a way, from the plastic film. It was not a heavy suit of armor but thin film which could be *dealt with using the tools at hand*.

I saw myself working in concert with Bob to let the old me die in reasonable comfort while at the same time freeing the other me to live life to its fullest.

Working toward Regression

My dread of getting into regression surfaced in nightly dreams which pushed R-day, regression day, into the future. My comments after one such dream where I was buying a car ran like this:

I'm not so sure deep down inside me but that therapy isn't another exercise in frustration. The car (therapy) looked good on the lot, but as I drive it around, I begin to wonder if it's anything at all. It was falling apart. The cost was more than its value to me.

I think the salesman's ultimate disinterest in me represents what I feel may be Bob's disinterest in me when he finally discovers I'm only kicking the tires and trying the doors of therapy, that deep down I don't have the where-withal to buy getting better.

I'm not sure if my determination not to buy the car (in the dream) was, as I think, a determination not to buy therapy.

On another night's dream, the interpretation read:

> This is my frustration expressed. I'm not positive where I'm going. I'm not sure I'm getting my money's worth in therapy. Nothing seems to be happening except that life is becoming more complicated and harder to figure out. Things—ideas and events—whiz by and crash; there are no clear tracks to follow; I don't have an identifiable destination; I change interim destinations constantly . The hopes of getting somewhere may be fading. In the series of dreams, I wind up having lost everything and I'm walking to nowhere.

Hope amid Impending Gloom

The stress was building ever higher. There was within me a terrible tug of war going on. I wanted to get better, which is to say I wanted to survive, but there was also an overwhelming desire not to have to face myself in therapy. The emotional hot and cold flashes kept me constantly off balance. I would make the definitive decision to push on, only to follow with the definitive decision to let well enough alone.

There was no end to the list of rationalizations on both sides of the argument. Chief among my reasons for not pushing on was my poor memory. I was afraid I would inadvertently make up stories to accommodate Bob, or that I might actually remember things I couldn't bring myself to say.

This led to a curious and hopeful train of thought which I recorded in the journal.

> Yesterday morning I thought of something shortly after I awakened and decided I would consider it during the commute to work. But during the commute I could not remember what it was. That has bothered me for the last twenty-four hours because it was something I wanted to think through.
>
> I remembered it walking into work today. It is this:
>
> I have some concerns about the regression exercise, one of them being that I wonder if there really *are* memories

locked inside my brain or if my brain never recorded many incidents. The evidence is how little I can recall compared to how much I want to have a good memory.

Now as I read a dream recorded in my journal, I find I'm surprised at how I can recall in rich detail the content of my dream. If I were to try to think of what I dreamed a night or two ago, or even last night, I wouldn't be able to tell you what it was, even though I had written it down. But when I *read* what I *wrote* upon awakening, much of the episode comes alive to me. I have vivid recall.

This suggests to me that there really are memories locked away, memories which *may* be recalled if the memory key is found to unlock the door of a given memory compartment. The trick is to find the key, to sidle up to the memories in a nonthreatening way and gain access. Once inside, I suspect that there may be significant detail available.

That is one hope. Another is that if this is true and it happens, the memory may contain keys to other memories, and a flood of connected events may pour out.

A second concern is that my memories may be so disconnected from each other, so insulated from their surroundings, that unless something *specific* brings them into view, they are for all practical purposes lost to me. I might only discover them by accident, as a builder might discover a treasure chest when he is digging foundations for a building.

Then, as I think back on my dream experiences, I remember the "something" that *does* bring back those dream memories: an urge to read what I dreamed last night so that I can tell someone about it. Maybe that will be applicable to regression.

Finally, even this itself—walking in this morning and suddenly thinking about the process which I could not remember at all yesterday and earlier this morning—happened not because my conscious mind was pushing for it. My conscious mind had given up remembering it. *It happened by itself.*

My mind, beneath the level of consciousness, had kicked this memory into the level of consciousness where it could be considered and used as a basis for further thinking.

I hesitate to say this is an encouraging sign. It may be a

fluke. At this moment it seems to be an encouraging sign, but years of experience indicate that later on today it won't seem that way.

But whether or not I emotionally accept it as an encouraging sign, *it happened and that is undeniable*. The fact that it happened is something I have to deal with . . . if I can remember to.

DR. RICHARD:

At the conclusion of the fourteenth session, I had completed an overview of Deacon's history. Additional revelations had shown a traumatic adolescence in addition to a destructive childhood. Even with what little Deacon could consciously recall, the review of his history stirred up much pain and distress. It was exceedingly difficult for him to delve into these areas which for so long had been avoided, denied, and presumably buried. But they were still very much *alive* as Deacon's emotions demonstrated.

The thought of regression to earlier life experiences was extremely disconcerting to Deacon. At that time he could not fathom how it would be to encounter such painful experiences. He wondered if he would survive, and he wondered if he could even respond to regression because of his "poor memory" and well-built defenses. Resistance to regression increased, but his dreams became open windows showing the intense struggle in his soul. His dreams at this time all had the common theme of growth versus no growth—should he continue running away or finally face himself in truth? Therapy could provide the answer, but at what price?

As a person begins to move more deeply toward confronting painful and hidden realities, resistances often multiply. Some persons may even balk at continuing and prematurely stop the process. By the seventeenth session Deacon was approaching a crisis, the resolution of which would determine whether he could or would continue. Not even I realized how intense the crisis was.

ANDERSON:

A Crisis Approaches

I was now approaching one of the most serious crises of my life and the roughest part of my experience in therapy. Intermingled with expressions of hope were expressions of despair and hopelessness. Two journal entries touch on my thought processes at the time. One has to do with my relationship with Mary, and the other with a midterm assessment of where I was in life.

DEFICIENCIES

This is a survey of my perceived deficiencies as a person, as I have come to accept them over the period of our marriage. It is not a comprehensive study of our relationship. It deals only with perceived deficiencies.

My deficiencies, as I interpreted by the reaction to me of the person most important to me, began to clarify after three months of marriage. By that time I had discovered that my wife had a distinct distaste for me, a distaste which bordered on repulsion.

—She did not care to touch me. Rarely, if ever, did she initiate contact.

—She would not of her own choice lie next to me.

—She did not sit next to me (i.e., in the car or on the couch) of her own volition.

—She would accept my holding her hand or arm when walking, but did not seek such contact.

—She rarely, if ever, indicated a desire to be touched or even admired by me.

—In the first two thirds or more of our marriage, my wife rarely, if ever, said, "I love you," except in response to such a statement from me.

The absence of my personal worth and value to my wife came into perspective when our children came. Her affection for them was wide open, constant, physical, and entirely public. The legitimate pride and admiration she had for them was in sharp contrast to the virtually total absence of any expression of pride, admiration, or affection for me.

—My person was not admired. I was neither handsome nor ugly.

—I excelled at nothing (and did badly at nothing).
I wasn't a good (or bad) writer.
I didn't have a good (or bad) voice.
I wasn't any kind of musician.
I was neither a good nor a bad provider.
I wasn't a good (or bad) reporter or editor.
I wasn't a good (or a bad) husband.

—My jokes were not funny.

—And always, always, always my judgments were especially (and probably genuinely) suspect.

All of this is also in sharp contrast to my view of my wife. She was and is beautiful, competent, spirited, and a great mother. She "feels good" to touch. She is a fantastic cook, seamstress, decorator, hostess, and organizer—the ultimate bookkeeper. She has uncommon common sense and more constructive energy than three normal people. Anything she puts on looks classic on her. She is the ideal mother-in-law to our children's spouses.

From the down payment on our first house to our vacations and putting the children in school or in houses, it is my wife's money, not mine, which allows us pleasures, while my money goes for maintenance.

While I am sure that my wife appreciated my view of her, there was nothing reciprocal in our relationship. That is to say, my admiration for her did not inspire returned appreciation.

Even to this day I don't know if my wife thinks I have a good singing voice. I can only contrast it to her often-expressed desire to hear our daughter sing and play the piano. This absence of interest quite well personifies why I feel deficient as a man and husband. I cannot make her happy. My sorriest effort is in the area of growing roses, which she loves and for which I have no talent.

In short, my interests do not contribute to our marriage, our family, or to our welfare.

These are my deficiencies as a person and husband. The absence of other, legitimate options is why I am tolerated or endured as a husband.

In discussing these observations with Bob, he noted that I had often said in earlier sessions that Dad "tolerated" me as a child. It is interesting to note that here I said, "I am tolerated or endured as a husband." It has the same ring, hasn't it?

A dream I had just before the crisis struck seemed to pull together what I was experiencing.

I started driving. It was farm country with rolling hills, and the road was of good gravel. Gradually the gravel gave way, and the road became more primitive until it was two ruts that I was following, not a gravel road. I first became confused, then wholly lost. I drove west all of the time.

After a very long time, the road became so poor that the car got stuck in a rut. Rather than seek help, I got out and started walking west. The road was terrible now. Even walking was difficult. In a dip in the road a short distance ahead of me, I saw two, then three, then several more very big, black, fierce dogs. I wondered where I was, where I could find help, whether those dogs were really fierce or whether I could bluff my way past them. I now realized I was completely, totally lost, and that I had lost the car as well. I had no idea where it was.

One of the dogs spotted me, and then the others saw me and began to come toward me, slowly and tentatively at first, and then they began to lope. I decided to turn around and get out of there fast, and then I realized my predicament. I didn't know where I was. I had nothing with which to defend myself. I had no place to go, no place where I would be safe.

I started to run, and then stopped running, and in a wave of discouragement and despair just walked slowly east, waiting for the dogs to catch up to me. At this point, the alarm clock went off, and I was greatly relieved.

This was a very frightening and depressing dream. It clearly indicates that I am wandering around trying to find my way to reality.

Is it possible that the car represented the therapy process? If so, it may be that I'm concerned that we're coming into a desolate place, that we're going to get stuck, and that I'm going to be all alone and defenseless when the wolves come to devour me.

Even now, as I copy these words for this book, I am touched by the sheer helplessness of the dream. I vividly remember the terror that possessed me. Something inside me was telling me there was no way out. I was going to be torn apart very soon. What a sad waste of a life.

DR. RICHARD:

As Deacon continued to open up to himself, his awareness of what he labeled as his "deficiencies" became increasingly acute. He was sensitive particularly to how his wife responded (or didn't respond) to him and interpreted her actions as a rejection of his person. The parallels between the lack of affirmation from his father and what he felt he was not getting from his wife were obvious. These problems in the marital relationship only served as further confirmation of his perceived worthlessness. His wife was wonderful, but he was *terrible*. The patterns learned in childhood were continuing to be played out in Deacon's head with devastating consequences.

Deacon's dream was a graphic symbolic representation of his emotional state. As he traveled down the therapeutic road on his journey inward, *his customary ways of approaching the world were beginning to collapse,* leaving him with a profound sense of lostness and a soul-penetrating fear. *Now no place was safe.* He really could not return to where he had come from, for he had already come too far. But he could not see his way beyond where he presently was. It seemed like the end—a terrifying and helpless place to be.

Profound psychological change always requires the demise of familiar but destructive patterns of thinking, feeling, and behaving. The collapse of these patterns is necessary so that healthier, more reality-oriented patterns may take their place. However, as this transformation begins, the client will frequently feel a terrifying sense of lostness. This is what I call the therapeutic "no man's land." It is the psychological void one experiences when the old is beginning to pass away, but the new has not yet emerged. Turning loose of the familiar, even though it is destructive, is a frightening experience, especially when it appears there is nothing to take its place. It is a time when one must press on to allow the new to emerge—which it does, sometimes at a painfully slow pace, but other times with surprising rapidity. Deacon was coming to his "no man's land" and was sure he would be devoured by it.

ANDERSON:

> "I'm really fed up."
> "I'm really depressed."

The Saturday session which preceded those despondent exclamations in my journal had been a downer, in keeping with the rest of the week. A family member driving our new car with only 660 miles on it had rear-ended a new Porsche—which was standing at a stop sign, no less. Later Mary and I had gotten into a charged discussion about the amount of my salary I was putting into savings. "I'm still a resource to her," I wrote, "and not much more."

The morning seemed to last forever. It felt like every hour had 180 minutes in it, and with each of them my spirit sank lower and lower. I had the sensation of listening to the ominous tick of a time bomb as it counted down the final seconds. Bizarre thoughts surged through my overheated mind, and by the middle of the day, I poured out my feelings to the journal.

> I'm in a blue funk. I am so very depressed I'm not sure I have the stuff to survive the day. I'm so tired.
> At fifty-six, what have I got? A wife who doesn't much like me. Kids who are wonderful but don't understand me.
> I have not a friend or confidant in the world—I never have had the latter. I have nothing to look forward to but old age alone, and it's setting in right now. I make money and it's gone. Mary would only be happy if I saved more than I make every year and never spent a cent of it so it would all be available to her after I die.
> I want to quit. Now. Right now. I want to kick it all over and quit. I can see no reason not to. Why keep up the charade? Whether I brought what I am on myself or not, whether or not I perpetuated it—no matter what, I still haven't got anything to look forward to, so why bother going forward?
> I want to die. Now.
> Life is not fun. It's just barely tolerable.
> Shall I bother to arrange the details that will have to be dealt with when I die? Like, show Mary the key to the bottom drawer at work where our papers are kept?
> My loss seems total. I can't think of anything that I want that I can have. I am very sick. I am going to die without

ever having known what it is to be unreservedly loved for who I am, damn me.

I loathe me. What has happened has happened. What is now is unsatisfying. What will be is boredom and insanity. Why is it I don't want to hurt the family by simply taking my life? I fear death a lot less today than I have in the past. The thought of no longer being tired is so tempting.

My heart is pounding dangerously hard. It actually hurts.

If something happens and I die, I hope Bob understands that I really appreciated his efforts toward me. It was just that I was too far gone when I reached out for help.

I am a dead man.

I think Mary wants me dead so she can concentrate on her friends. Why not?

Here the journal entry just stops. My brain was a roller coaster accelerating on desperately sad memories, expired hopes, and dismal projections. My dreams were gone. So, God loved me? All right, I could accept that, though for the life of me—literally—I couldn't think why he did. *So what?* I asked myself, in despair rather than arrogance. So what difference does it make to me or others that God loves me?

In those infernal hours, my energy level fell so low I really did believe I might well die that night, die from sheer fatigue and tiredness. It is a tiresome cliché, but there was no longer a light at the end of the tunnel—only death. Nothing made sense anymore, and I could no longer write, or talk, or even think rationally.

DR. RICHARD:

In the Saturday session to which Deacon refers, I observed that he was very discouraged. Indeed, he was wondering if therapy was working. Would he ever get to the side of feeling emotionally healthy? He felt unsupported by his wife (or anyone for that matter), and the crucial experience of self-love and self-nurturing was absent. At this point in his treatment, Deacon evidenced all the symptoms of profound depression: a lack of energy, a sense of nothing to look forward to, an urge to die, a keen sense of utter worthlessness. In short, life was completely shutting down for him.

This kind of intense depression can only be truly appreciated by those who have been through it. If there is a "living hell," then this must be it. No human being can exist in this state for long. Thus, such depression is often a precursor of change. It can also be a dangerous time. If a person's energy is high enough and he or she feels desperate enough, an actual attempt at suicide may occur.

I was concerned about Deacon, but I knew that he had been making progress (though he did not feel like it then). I also knew that we were about to start regression therapy, which undoubtedly was affecting his current emotional state. All in all, I felt a confidence that Deacon could genuinely begin to face himself and his past without ending his life. He would get through the psychological "no man's land." This was a clinical judgment of the kind all psychotherapists are called upon to make from time to time. Such judgments are based on complex factors that involve the clinician's training, experience, and intuitive sense of what is happening with the client.

ANDERSON:

It was another eight days before I could come back and write the following record of what happened during the terrible hours I now refer to as Black Sunday. I want to give you a slightly abridged but near verbatim account of that record. The account begins the day before Black Sunday.

TURNING POINT

Statements [made by Mary] triggered the reaction that set in immediately. I became very withdrawn. This added its own kind of stress. Our youngest son was leaving for college shortly, and I would only be with him on this weekend. I didn't want anything to mar the time nor the wonderful relationship that exists between him and me, but I was almost out of control. Fortunately, as it turned out, he was gone most of Saturday.

I began to come down hard on myself, really hard. I found no worth in me and decided that I had always and permanently missed my potential for worth. It was lost and not recoverable. I became extremely depressed.

Unannounced, I went for a long, slow walk, focusing on my morbid prospects. It affirmed I had no worth. On the walk I shambled by the home of a family-therapy counselor who attends our church just as he was driving out of his driveway. It jarred me back to the present for a moment, and I said hello. He smiled and then said he noticed "a terribly depressed man" walking past and was surprised to see it was me. It wasn't much as conversations go, but it endorsed the validity of my depression. The nearest thing to a bright spot for the day was the satisfaction of knowing I wasn't wearing a phony pleasant face.

Now I was beginning to think about suicide. I had never had the courage, if that is what it took, to give serious consideration to taking my own life. But that was changing now as I saw my life ending, whether I committed suicide or not.

The survival instinct kicked on and off. At moments I thought taking my life was a mind-set that would pass. Then I would assess what life would be like beyond the crisis: just what it had always been like. Or would it? I knew I was not being completely rational. When I arrived home from my walk, I took out pencil and paper to develop a list of things I looked forward to. After thirty minutes I had nothing on the list. There it was, blank evidence that I had nothing to look forward to. All of the pleasures I would enjoy in life had already been experienced, and even they had been rendered meager by my worthlessness.

Mary went somewhere—I later learned she went to pick up some things at a shopping center—and I thought, "Look at that! I'm glad in my black moment that she didn't interrupt me, but she knows how I feel, and even she doesn't think I'm worth interrupting. She could have said something." I went for a second long walk.

Thoughts of suicide began to have a life of their own—it became almost a given—and now I focused on how I could accomplish this death without distressing the family. Shooting would be bloody and gory, and besides I don't own a gun. Jumping off a bridge would be kind of distant and inconvenient—I don't own a bridge, either—and on the drive over, I might change my mind. And Mary would have to claim the car and view the body and such. No good.

At one point I wondered why I cared what the reaction would be. And then I had to face the fact that I did care.

I was also concerned about insurance. I was not sure if some clause in my policy would nullify or cut in half the benefits for Mary if I killed myself. Doing one's self in and sparing the family grief was a complicated business.

Finally I came upon the idea of not eating. I would simply not eat or drink, but I would do this in a way that wouldn't be obvious. In perhaps three weeks' time I would be gone. I could maybe induce my own kind of terminal anorexia. As I entered the house, it occurred to me that I was a social anorexic and had been one for a long time. I fairly much decided on that course of action.

Still, there was a problem. I didn't want to have my son start his first year away from home with something wrong. He had come home by now, and Mary had begun to fix dinner. It was not unusual for me to be reading when he came home, and he was so wrapped up in his own thoughts that my withdrawnness was pretty much lost on him.

At dinner I said I wasn't really hungry and only ate a token bit of meat, a couple of beans, and nothing else. Because of what was going on inside me, I was actually not hungry.

I went to bed early with only a minimum of conversation. I'm sure our son thought I was tired, which was certainly true. Tired, and terribly tense and stressed out. I even wrote "I'm a dead man" on the tablet upon which I had been trying to list future joys and hopes.

When Mary came to bed, I felt so miserable for her—

thinking she might be blaming herself for my problems—
that I told her that I wasn't angry with her, that I was en-
raged with myself and that I hated myself.

I slept okay and had a dream which is significant because,
for the first time in my dream life, I took charge of a situation and rebuffed the authority figure. (It is worth telling
here in the sequence it happened.)

The Dream

I was walking past a convalescent hospital wearing a
shirt and a pair of boxer shorts. For no discernible reason, I
decided to change to a new pair of shorts right there on the
sidewalk.

As I was in the process of changing, a big red-haired guy
on the other side of the street called to me. His voice charged
with amazement and indignation, he shouted, "You can't do
that here!" I felt that if I went through with the change, he
would come over and attack me or turn me in to the police or
something. I woke up immediately.

A few moments later, before I had shrugged away entirely the feeling of fear, I decided to try something Bob
had suggested about dreams; go back to sleep and alter the
dream to give a more satisfying ending. That's just what I
did, and it worked! (You could not be nearly as surprised as
I was.)

It was as though I started over at reel one. Everything
happened again as it happened in the first dream. At the
point in my dream where I was changing shorts, the man
appeared again, but this time instead of being across the
street, he was just ahead of me, cutting off my path. And
instead of being big, he was *huge*. "You can't do that!" he
said, with that indignant look on his face.

Now this is extraordinary. I knew I was dreaming, and I
felt authorized by Bob to decide to change the course of
the dream. With my heart in my throat, I mustered up the
courage to say back to him, "This is my dream. I can do
what I want in my dreams. If you want something different,

go have a dream of your own." And with that I began again to change shorts, watching him all the while. The enormous man sort of reared back, startled and confused. And then he wasn't there anymore. He just sort of disintegrated. I finished changing and went on. I woke up strangely satisfied—"strangely" because I was wholly unaware of the significant change which was going to occur in me later in the day.

DR. RICHARD:

As Deacon waged his intense internal struggle, he became aware that he did care how others would respond to his premature, self-inflicted demise. He was caught in a horrible conflict of wanting to do away with himself yet at the same time wanting somehow not to cause those close to him any pain—an impossibility. With his remaining rationality, Deacon believed there was no way out of that dilemma.

But there was a way out, and the answer came in a dream. The mind is one of God's most amazing creations. It is here within us that the most profound answers to the most crucial questions of life are resolved. There is no way in which we can predict precisely how, when, or in what way the answers may be forthcoming. For Deacon, his dream became both the playing field for and symbolization of a deep internal shift which resolved his dilemma. And what was this shift that made all the difference? Simply this: Deacon, using the vehicle of his dream, finally, in the depths of his being, took control of his own life. By "redreaming" the dream, he played out a scenario in which *he took charge and became the director of the dream rather than simply an actor in it.* And amazingly enough he found he could make a difference. The sense of powerlessness began to wane, an experience that would be repeated over and over again in regression therapy.

ANDERSON:

Black Sunday

I had no breakfast. I had had a minimal lunch and no dinner the night before, and yet I wasn't hungry. I was tension personified. When Mary got up, she hugged me hard and cried and said she wished I didn't have the pain I had. I was so emotionally spent by this time that I only wanted her to let me go. When she said she loved me, I told her to think about what she said, and said something to the effect that it was not good or reasonable to love s——. I don't think I had ever so much as used that word in front of her before.

We went to church and, in church, I began wondering about speeding up the death process after our son had left, by penetrating my heart with our biggest kitchen knife. Even during the sermon my right hand felt for the place in my rib cage which would allow me to reach the heart with one hard plunge. I hadn't decided to do this, but it had now become an option.

I sang no hymns. I read no Scripture. I heard very little outside what was going on in my head. We went to our adult class and there, strangely, I was warmed by the presentation, which was on love. Not heated, but warmed, and I was able to converse a little with Mary and our son on the way to lunch.

During the drive to the restaurant, our son asked if something was wrong. Mary said no, and I said I was extremely tired. He accepted that. At the restaurant I ordered only a bowl of soup, but I was beginning to have some reservations about the course I had chosen. Our table talk was almost normal.

I kept loosening up as the afternoon wore on, and by mid-afternoon the crisis had ended. I cannot explain this. I can only presume that my mind was weighing all the pros and cons, reflecting perhaps on the progress I had made in therapy. In any case, I made no conscious decision not to take my life. It just sort of happened. I walked into the kitchen and hugged Mary and said quietly that it was over.

She could hardly believe it. In fact, it was not until late Friday, five days later and after yet another session with Bob, that she could accept it fully.

A week later a not-so-subtle change has come over me. I feel like a different person! In some literal way I feel like the phony Deacon Anderson, the old one who lived life on false beliefs, really did die eight days ago and has been replaced by a new Deacon Anderson who has a very different mind-set.

I have miles to go yet. I must now work on regression therapy, going back to what I learned wrong and unlearning it. I recognize it will be full of pain, but I think it will be nothing like that which I have recently experienced. And I also know that facing this pain will bring healing and a better life.

I'm ready for that now. I'm ready for that.

DR. RICHARD:

"Black Sunday" saw Deacon emerge from the depths of his crisis. At a most profound and unconscious level, healing had begun. It was a small but extremely significant step which would lead to far-reaching changes as Deacon entered into regression therapy. Indeed, this initial step toward healing laid the foundation upon which regression therapy could further build and energize the healing process.

In sessions eighteen and nineteen, following Black Sunday, Deacon shed many tears, but he also exuded an excitement about the changes he was experiencing inside. He found himself continuing to take charge in his dreams, vanquishing any obstacles which were in his way. This new power uplifted him, and he was now able to consider the prospect of facing his past with a strength he had never possessed before. He knew it would be tough, but he also knew he had turned the corner and was emerging from his private psychological hell.

V.

THE EMERGENCE

A new life takes form

When I was a child, I talked like a child, I thought like a child, I reasoned like a child. When I become a [56-year-old] * man, I put childish ways behind me.

—1 Corinthians 13:11, NIV

ANDERSON:

Regression played such a substantive role in my healing that I want to spend a bit of time talking about it. Coming into therapy, I held the notion that regression was some kind of psychological hocus-pocus, a therapeutic trick done with mental mirrors. I wanted none of it. It was in no little part the dread of regression that put me under the intense stress which triggered Black Sunday.

Perhaps in any therapy, certainly in mine, regression is the most painful tool in the therapist's kit. I liked nothing about it. Even the sound of the word—*regression*—is

---

* This bracketed insert shows how Deacon personalizes Scripture when he reads it. It has been his lifelong practice to read his current circumstances into Scripture to get a better understanding of its contemporary application.

charged with foreboding. It was progress I wanted, not regress. I wanted to go forward, not go back to the very life experiences I was trying to get away from.

My reluctance about regression therapy was neither superficial nor trivial. It was a carefully reasoned stance, seasoned over time and tailored to protect me from the terrible secrets of my life. Had I learned life wrong? *No, I reasoned, I had not. It was life that was wrong, not me!* My perceptions of life were encased in an almost impenetrable strata of tightly compressed emotional experiences, each memory and its attendant feelings locking arms with the ones above and beneath to rebuff any insinuation that digging into the archives of emotional experience was a reasonable course of action for any purpose. Maybe it was appropriate in the lives of others. Maybe it even worked for them. In my case —no! I think now my inflexible position was the product of the pain that I was certain would accompany regression. I was right about that.

Bob addressed the subject head-on. Surgery hurts, he said. And there would be no anesthetic to dull the pain of regression. It would be necessary to be aware of the pain so I could help Bob guide the scalpel as he probed my mind and scraped long dormant memories back into consciousness where I could deal with them.

I found regression to be a kindred experience to paying a visit to the suburbs of hell. It hurt to drive the wedge of conscious awareness between those compressed layers I relied on to keep life at arm's distance. In tracking down the origins of my emotional cancers, we exhumed fetid memories and poked through old transactions. And the pain of discovery was as devastating as the false premises upon which I had built my life. It was terrible.

It was also entirely worth it. It was, in fact, essential to the work of rooting out the wrong presumptions which had ruined my life.

Bottled up inside were misshapen concepts about myself

and the world about me, concepts formed in the malleable years of childhood, concepts based upon regrettable family circumstances as interpreted by a five-year-old who new no other norm. Before I could say *repression*, let alone know what it meant, the events of life were so painful, so condemnatory, that I jammed the cork into the neck of the memory bottle after each event. It took all my strength to keep the bottle corked during all the subsequent years. No wonder I was forever tired. No wonder I had no strength left to deal with what was going on outside of me.

Bob approached regression in a nonthreatening way, never forcing the issue but frequently referring to the benefits that would follow. I had profited from the new understandings of myself to the point that I finally put my trust in Bob on the matter of regression. Whatever the outcome, I was willing to let regression work its painful work in me. Bob had used relaxation exercises earlier. Although I had been reluctant to try them, the relaxation exercises worked —spectacularly in some instances—and those successes helped me face regression.

The pressure from the fetid boil of pain which had been trickling emotional poison into my mental bloodstream over the years had become so great that my waning strength could no longer contain it. If memory serves me correctly, the first hour of regression blasted the cork to smithereens. Years and years and years of pain came gushing out in hot tears which would not be dammed. I tried. I still tried to keep it in, but I could not, any more than Mount Etna could contain the burst of lava. Wave after wave of molten emotion racked me, expressed in tears and sweat, releasing the pain which had all of my life influenced so much of how I faced life. How good it felt to cry—at last. And when the outburst subsided, an incredible sensation of relief and peace flooded through my entire being. It wasn't me that was wrong. It was what I had learned that was wrong.

DR. RICHARD:

Many clients have questions and fears concerning regression therapy. While regression therapy is not appropriate for many persons, it is very helpful to those who have had difficult or traumatic childhoods, particularly when there has been physical and/or sexual abuse.

Before beginning this procedure with anyone, I try to explain clearly what I will be doing and why I feel it is needed. There are various forms of therapy that utilize the principle of regression, which basically means taking a person back to a previous life experience that was emotionally significant for him or her. In some cases these life experiences are so repressed that the client cannot consciously bring them to awareness. Regression allows an individual to begin to penetrate the barriers of repression and see anew and reexperience early events or patterns of behavior which have been lost to consciousness, but which have profoundly affected later adult life.

Experiencing a regressed state is not like remembering a past event. It is much more like being there again. Not only does one have images of the long-repressed event or behavior, but one also can begin to feel directly the emotions surrounding the experience, and sometimes even feel specific sensations in the body which were associated with the event. The emotions and bodily sensations have been buried right along with the visual perception of what happened, and in an effective regression it all begins to come out together. As one might imagine, regression can be an extraordinarily painful process as an individual comes face to face with experiences now surfacing after years of being either totally out of consciousness, or lodged in some dim awareness. Even if the experience is quite available to consciousness, regression can still be painful because it presents one with a quality of "being there" again rather than simply recalling to mind.

In working with many individuals over the years, I had found that, while regression produced considerable emotional catharsis (that is, a cleaning out of emotional debris associated with early life trauma) and much new awareness, neither the catharsis nor the new awareness were enough to bring about the level of healing necessary to get the client clear of his or her damaged past. Indeed, I felt something more was needed, but what?

Listening closely to clients' reports, I learned that the single most common experience they had when regressed to childhood trauma was a feeling of utter powerlessness and helplessness (with an accompanying sense of fear and anger). Returning again to a childhood state of consciousness makes the sense of being overwhelmed by a parent or other adult most vivid.

It seemed likely to me that if the regressed individual could be assisted to feel less helpless and powerless, the trauma of the original experience might be greatly modified. From this surmise came the notion of restructuring early experiences through regression. Thus regression therapy not only takes the client back to the original experience, but it helps him or her to relive it with a whole different scenario and outcome in mind. This new scenario puts the regressed person into a position of increased power and less helplessness in the presence of the intimidating adult. For example, when a person is regressed to an event of abuse experienced in childhood, he or she is then encouraged to say to the offending adult what he or she really feels.

In other words, the client "rewrites" the script so that it comes out with him or her feeling much more powerful in the situation. The result is different from what was experienced in the original encounter. But often it is necessary to engage repeatedly in regression/restructuring involving the same or similar scenes with the offending adult (or other significant person in the child's life—sometimes it is a sibling). As the regression and restructuring therapy proceeds, the actual perceptions and emotions surrounding the traumatic event are altered. The emotional charge is diminished and the sense of powerlessness and helplessness fades. In other words, the entire traumatic event (or events) seems to dramatically lose its power in the client's life, and in doing so, affects many other client responses and self-perceptions which have grown out of or have been shaped by the early trauma.

This is similar to the "pebble in the pond" effect. When a pebble is dropped in a mirror-smooth pond, the ripples from it may be seen extending across the pond. The whole pond is affected in some measure by the dropping of that pebble. Similarly, when early trauma is later treated by regression and restucturing, the entire person is affected in various ways and at various levels.

The results of this kind of therapy often seem amazing to the client. Not only are symptoms significantly reduced or eliminated altogether, but behaviors and feelings which heretofore have seemed quite perplexing are understood with a clarity never before experienced. Indeed, as one emerges from this therapy process, there is often a deep sense of having been healed. Deacon's response is very much to the point: *He* wasn't wrong; it was how he had learned to experience himself and the world that was wrong. Regression therapy brought the profound realization of that truth to Deacon in a way that nothing else could.

ANDERSON:

Repression and Regression

In a typical regression I would return to an event involving my father. To say that my father was the towering authority figure in my life is to say Mount Everest is "fairly big." My father was the Omnipotent Ruler of All the World, the setter of all standards of conduct for all of life, the arbiter of all issues. His all-powerful hands had the capacity to sting, to maim, to beat down, to squeeze out. Through regression I realized that the way I knew he had the capacity for cruelty was by his proclivity to engage in it.

Others who knew him knew a very different person—one that was kind and self-sacrificing to the extreme. He may have been that to them. He may even have been that to me. (I don't for a moment think he was, but he *may* have been.) What is important, what is pertinent, is *how I perceived him to be.*

Dad never exhibited warm or tender feelings for me— when he noticed me at all. He generally ignored me.

On those occasions when Dad gave specific recognition to things I had done, it was only in the form of criticism, condemnation, or outright corporal punishment. With childish logic, I decided that universally unworthy actions must be the product of universally unworthy people. A child of two or three or four doesn't have enough social experience to know that fathers sometimes make mistakes, or that they may be emotionally troubled, or that other children who do the same things gain different responses from their fathers. I concluded very early on that I was not like the rest of the world—I was unworthy. An unworthy three-year-old!

At three, what I wanted more than anything else in life was not a toy or friends. My fondest practical hope was to not be noticed in any way by my father. I yearned for Dad not to think about me. Of course, a three-year-old really needs a father, and I was no exception. But I was so afraid of Dad that I didn't dare to be around him. He knew what a bad person I was, and he had to correct me through punishment.

It is a terrible irony, but in order to simply survive at all in the world in which I found myself, I had to appear not to be in any kind of trouble at all. I had to appear that way to everyone. If I conformed in everything, I might manage to evade for a little longer the exposure of my "wrongdoing" and the punishment that I must deserve and that would surely come.

To conform in everything, I had to learn to be invisible, and I did it well. I learned how to not be noticed, to move without sound, to not look people in the eye, to never raise my voice for any reason, to walk softly, to play quietly, to sit very still, to suffer without complaint, and to smile when anyone looked at me. I gave it my full attention and generally performed as a master actor. Yet, to be ignored is the cruelest cut of all. To not be worth noticing is to be evaluated as something less than fully human. Had my father sought me out and punished me to improve me, I would have seen myself as someone worth improving. Not once, insofar as I can remember, was that even a remote motivation.

Very early on my whole being began to shriek silently— the only way allowed—for help. People felt sorry for the five-year-old who had debilitating headaches once or twice a week. In the early stages of these headaches came nausea, followed by vomiting. Then the throbbing in my brain cage would begin. It battered away at my senses until finally I had to lie on my back, eyes closed to all light, to see the red and black tracings on my closed eyelids. Pain eventually rendered me utterly helpless. I could not move my head. I could talk to no one, eat or drink nothing, listen to nothing. My neck and shoulder muscles would stiffen and ache from holding my head rigidly still. Even so at times it seemed as if the top of my head would explode. Surely there must be a stronger label than *migraine* to describe such episodes.

Hours later I would sink into the sleep born of total exhaustion. The next morning, I would awaken in shaky health to face another day. If my father noticed me at all at the breakfast table, it would be with a baleful glance which said to me, "Why did I have to have a weakling son like this?"

The migraine headaches were the product of stress built up by the tremendous effort necessary to remain invisible, obedient, conforming, all the while knowing I was the

Unworthy One. They were a result of the clash between the real world and the inappropriate self-image which possessed me.

I could not always succeed in being invisible. As a result, Dad spanked me frequently and severely, sometimes maniacally.

As a four-year-old, I had no way of knowing that Dad was a troubled man. I knew only that my father was the pastor, the man of God, the man who could do no wrong. Obviously, I must be the transgressor. I had sinned. I had done wrong. I deserved punishment. Never for a moment did I feel I did not have coming to me all that I frequently got. I was worthless. I was an embarrassment to my father. Because I had some terrible defect, I could do nothing right.

And I had repeated, painful evidence of that. I tried to do everything right, but I got punished for everything I did or did not do. And, as I saw it, deservedly so. Dad, who understood life, would not have been driven to administer such pain if I had not been terribly bad.

Even as I write this, I cannot help but get tears in my eyes for that poor little guy who wanted so much to do the right things, to please his father, who tried so very hard with every ounce of strength he had in him to be a good child. And I get angry, too. I know that it was not a mean little boy who was punished for doing wrong. I am incensed that a 190-pound man would inflict severe corporal punishment on an essentially innocent child who weighed maybe forty pounds. Even if he was troubled, how could he do it? My system cries out in grief and rage.

I could at times spill out some of my pain to my mother, who nourished me with unlimited tender love. Unfortunately, Mom was as much in the conformity box as I was.

Never once did Mom intervene to end or ease my punishment. Not once did she even protest, although her eyes, too, were filled with quiet tears. Mom was my nourisher. I think she loved me more than life itself, but she was no match for my father. She knew, as I know now, that he would not for a second have tolerated any interference from Mom. Standing under five-feet tall and probably weighing ninety-five pounds soaking wet and shy and timid by nature, Mom was just not up to interfering. Still I get angry. How could anyone, and especially a mother, stand by and see her child tortured in the way I was tortured in the name of punishment? Did she not want to diminish my need for her post-torture nourishment? To this day, I can't quite understand it.

As part of regression therapy, I came to realize that the very fact of Mom's not interfering was taken by me as validating my father's opinion of my worthlessness. I'm touched today by the fact that it made me love her more for being able to love and be kind to someone as stupid and bad as I.

So, these were the kinds of things that regression brought to the surface. These things I did not want to dredge up into my consciousness; I didn't want to deal with them. And I didn't want to disclose to Bob (or anyone) what kind of a rotten person I really was under my polite smile.

Now, when I weep, I weep not for a bad child but for the child whose childhood and much of his adult life was snuffed out because he misunderstood things about himself, and to a lesser degree for a mother who was a precious and loveable wimp, and for a father who was never quite at peace with himself and never at all at peace with his son. I weep for Dad because he missed a lot, too. He never knew he had given birth to a neat kid.

I often wept as I drove home from a therapy session. On one instance I wept so intensely that I thought I would have to park and drive home in stages. Regression was a form of dying in the hope of rising again as a new person This is not a spiritual statement, but the parallel is in some ways amazingly similar. It was ridding myself of some inappropriate mind-sets which fettered me. It was the leveling of the playing field to start a new game. Regression was the price of redemption.

In summary, through regression I picked through the most painful shards of a shattered childhood and youth. What I was doing was more than just remembering. I was coming to a new understanding that I had made some wrong, if innocent, conclusions about myself and my worth. My childhood environment made other choices remote at best, and while that is interesting and unfortunate, it doesn't alter that fact that I did make wrong conclusions about my worth—conclusions I lived by as gospel in my adult years.

Now with more strength and maturity than I had at three, I was able to revise my choices about myself, bringing them in line with reality. I was able to come to a new and more accurate understanding of the authority figure who did so much to shape—or misshape—how I experienced life.

What is said in such a brief space here took weeks of twice-a-week sessions with Bob. If I had the power to write with all the emotion I experienced in those sessions, this page would curl up from the heat. The pain-filled labyrinth of misunderstandings yielded slowly, *but it yielded.* Praise God!

DR. RICHARD:

The early stages of regression therapy focused on the first authority figure and person of power in Deacon's life—his father. Now Deacon was confronting his father as a child, but not in a position of powerlessness. Now he could see so clearly how very disturbed his father was, and he also could do something about it while in a state of regression. There were several scenarios in which Deacon faced his father.

I well recall the first regression when Deacon relived an experience he had had at age three. His father was verbally abusing Deacon and his sister, and I asked Deacon to tell his father what he really was feeling about this abuse. Deacon seemed to freeze in fear.

"No," he said, "I can't do that."

"Yes, you can, Deacon," I replied firmly.

"No, I can't," he shot back. Then there was a pause.

Finally, from the depths of his struggle, he told his father to stop his verbal lashing and to leave him and his sister alone. He spoke moderately but definitely, and then he saw himself turn and walk away. To his amazement, his father left him alone. Out of this first fearful "encounter" with his father, a new sense of confidence began to emerge.

A second and very significant regression occurred about two weeks later. Deacon regressed to age four, and his mind led him to an incident which happened in church, where his father publicly embarrassed him in front of the congregation by scolding him from the pulpit. Then he saw himself at home with his father who was sitting across from him threatening to beat him with a paddle should Deacon misbehave in church again.

Deacon felt so afraid and so helpless, but, at my suggestion, he began to face his father. He began to make his father visually smaller—he literally shrank him in physical size—and then began to pour out years of accumulated anger. He concluded by saying he wanted to wash out his father's mouth with soap and spank him! The father simply sat there, dumbfounded, and remained small. Following this regression, Deacon had an incredible feeling of freedom. For the first time in his life, he was truly beginning to free himself emotionally from his father's tyranny.

Regressions involving Deacon's father continued for several sessions. There were also some regressions in which Deacon confronted his mother about her lack of dealing with his father. These released further feelings of frustration and anger.

As we progressed, Deacon's confidence grew, and his newfound freedom was at times exhilarating. Increasingly he felt more at ease with others, he shared much more with his wife, and even confronted a boss at work. Increased confidence and a sense of freedom are often prominent experiences in regression therapy. Once this feeling of freedom and confidence begins to happen, the whole process takes on a self-reinforcing aspect as the client can now see clearly how it is beginning to directly benefit his or her life. The initial fears evaporate, and in their place often comes an attitude of, "I don't enjoy it, but it's really helping, so let's get on with it."

ANDERSON:

Affirming Dreams

As I began to find my psychological footing, my dreams began to mirror the powerful changes that were taking place within me.

Two months after Black Sunday, I peopled a dream with a father in his sixties, his son in his thirties, and me. I became aware that the pair were conferring quietly about how they might kill me. The son turned toward me with a sword in his hands, and I knew that if he got the chance to lift the blade up, I was a goner. I had in hand a pair of scissors, so I lunged out and stabbed him several times.

I whirled around to face the father, who now looked confused. Taking advantage of his moment of perplexion, I leaped at him and plunged the scissors into his chest several times. He staggered away, and I knew he, too, was dying. Then I stabbed myself, but my target was the right side of my chest, away from my heart. I woke up feeling really good about what had happened.

Later, after discussing it with Bob, I came to believe that the father in the dream was my father and his son was me prior to the time I came into freedom from the tyranny of my father. The son was the old Deacon, still acting in the context of his childhood belief system. It was this belief system I had put to death.

When I stabbed myself in a nonfatal place, it probably suggested that therapy was still in progress, that there were more events to be dealt with, more new understandings to be gained.

DR. RICHARD:

As we have seen, dreams reflect our emotional condition with uncanny accuracy. Moving along in therapy, Deacon continued to record, and we continued to reflect upon, dreams he was having, especially those that seemed directly connected to what was happening in the regression therapy. Power over his father's tyranny and over the "old Deacon" was clearly ascending, and it would never be lost.

ANDERSON:

Adolescence and Intimacy

Although a person may have little sense of self-worth and extremely low self-esteem, he or she still has the fundamental human need for intimacy. I had a special closeness with my mother as a child, but as the years rolled on, I became ever less involved with other people, including Mom. At an age when most kids are cultivating a circle of friends, I felt unworthy to be with others and always hung around on the fringes. I was afraid others might see through the veneer of my smile and penetrate the wit which I used to entertain others and keep them at arm's distance.

When I did reach out, it was often to other disadvantaged people—other loners desperately needing companionship.

But being together with other people who also had emotional problems did not make for satisfying companionships. There was a kind of sourness in knowing that the primary ingredient in our friendship was the feeling of being inferior to other people.

For example, there was the time when another high school outsider and I went joyriding. In those days people often left their keys in the cars, and it was easy to slip in, drive around awhile and return the car to where we found it. We finally got caught, of course, but the officer was kindly, and we had done no damage to the cars. To damage anything would have been wholly out of keeping with my personality.

As the new me emerged, I came to recognize I didn't go joyriding for the fun of driving or riding in a car. I wanted to have a close, personal relationship with another human being, and the ne'er-do-well son of the town character was as hungry for an intimate connection as I was. Both of us—I from the higher strata of town society, the son of a pastor, and he from society's basement—were just terribly lonely kids. It was solely our loneliness that drove us together.

Our association fell apart when my compadre tried to con me into purse stealing. I didn't actually steal any purses. He did. And then he brought them to where we had agreed to meet, but I could not bring myself to share in the booty. After that meeting, he went one way and I went another. Within a year he was in a reform school. We had a brief reunion after he was released and even celebrated it by going on one more joyride. But it was a sad attempt to resurrect something that never was, and we both knew it. He left town that night, a sad and lonely fifteen-year-old who would be killed in a fight before he was even out of his teens.

There were other similarly unhealthy temporary alliances. My hunger for acceptance was probably so palpable it drove most people away before I could manage to form any long-term relationships in high school or college.

DR. RICHARD:

As one might expect, an unhealthy childhood does not a healthy adolescence make. Deacon brought a conglomerate of problems with him into his teenage years, not the least of which was a failure to achieve any kind of close relationships with peers. Deacon's childhood traumas had blocked him from developing normally in adolescence. Now we used regression therapy to go back to his adolescence and restucture some particularly painful and demeaning episodes involving his father, other adults, and peers. While these incidents were more available to Deacon's consciousness, he had never faced them in the manner allowed by regression therapy, nor had he been able to achieve any sense of power over them prior to this time.

ANDERSON:

A New Mood

The weeks following Black Sunday, though made difficult by the necessary regression exercises, were also times of prodigious growth. As my view of myself shifted, my view of everything and everyone else began to change as well. People became interesting as individuals. I saw them in the richness of their beings; their hopes and aspirations, their victories and failures became fascinating. I no longer needed to hide, because now I liked who I was, and that made a very great difference in how I related to others.

I continued to think long and deep about my dad, and my mother, and concluded that they, too, had been very troubled people but without the advantages that therapy now offered to their offspring. I have been able to accept them for who they were, forgive them for what they did, and acknowledge that I will never comprehend the forces which shaped them and brought these two lonely people together for life.

Dad mellowed some in his later years, but never really came to know what it was to relax and let other people be themselves, to enjoy other people for who they are. Mom remained precious and dear and kind, but was to her last days concerned about what others might think of her.

Session by session old buried concepts were disinterred, dusted off, and dealt with. Prospects for life became brighter and brighter. I was having fun. The relationship between Mary and me had never been as good as it had come to be during this period.

Three months after Black Sunday I had a dream in which I had gone to Canada for some reason. Coming back, I stopped at the border and turned in Canadian money for U.S. money. I didn't have much to convert, and I was astounded when the customs agent pushed over the counter a humongous stack of American bills. The dream ended as I crossed into the U.S., flabbergasted at my good fortune and looking forward to showing Mary how well I had done.

I interpreted that to mean I had lived temporarily, even if for a long time, in a foreign country where I had little currency to spend. Now, at last, I was coming home and swapping my puny earnings for a fortune. The immense return represented how fortunate I now felt to be who I was and where I was in life. I felt equipped to live life in a rich and satisfying way, no longer having to eke by on a meager mental budget. I could ante up and play the game with anyone.

The best way to describe the pre- and post- Black Sunday experience is to say my life took on a brand-new tone. Instead of anticipating defeat, I expected to win.

A Round-up of Changes

In the last verse of the apostle John's account of the life of Christ (21:25, NIV), he observes that Jesus did so many things other than those in his account that "even the whole world would not have room for the books" which would be necessary to record everything. I have that same feeling about the changes in my life that have come about through therapy.

So many things transpired on so many levels of my life that in many ways I was no longer the same person who dragged himself kicking and screaming into therapy. Four months after Black Sunday I felt like a new person. At age fifty-six I had wondered if I had enough of life left to be worth risking a therapeutic salvage mission. At fifty-seven I had the powerful answer—Yes!

I was the old Deacon Anderson turned inside out. Life was no longer a chore to be endured. It was interesting and exciting. At last I was interested in uncovering things about myself because I could view them in a sympathetic mental environment. I came to understand why I thought and acted as I did, and when I found such thoughts or actions inappropriate to the situation I faced, I could change. (This is so easy to write now, but I remember it was impossible to even think of fundamental changes before therapy. At that point I was convinced that things were as things were and that was that, and I was stuck with it.)

As I discovered new things about myself, I found I was also learning new things about the world I lived in. Before therapy I could not appreciate the environment surrounding me because everything was a threat to me. I measured everything by its degree of danger to my way of thinking and acted accordingly. Every moment, even in my dreams, I was judged by who or what was around me. In turn, I judged my environment. Therapy shriveled this attitude, and I began for the first time in my entire life to enjoy who I was, where I was. Instead of being threatened by the situations in which I found myself, I came to savor them. Take, for instance, the matter of driving in the car.

One of the "accomplishments" I trotted out regularly to

prove my worth was that on several driving trips from California to the Midwest and back, I was only passed once, and that was in the middle of the night in Nevada by a Cadillac traveling faster than 100 miles an hour. I saw no scenery on those cross-country treks. I saw only life in the rearview mirror as I looked out for patrol cars. As a lifelong commuter, I used to brag that I was the first person to reach San Francisco every day. It was a way of saying that no one ever passed me on the way to San Francisco. Alas, it was true.

Without once addressing it, therapy wrought an incredible change in my lifelong driving habits. Someone at work mentioned that instead of listening to the all-news station for traffic reports and other software of life, a driver who wanted to live a little longer and enjoy his commute should resolve to stay in the slow right-hand lane for his entire trip and to listen to a classical-music station. I had never done either of these things.

So one day I tuned in a classical-music station and pulled into the right-hand lane, and I have been there ever since. It is not an exercise in discipline. It is an exercise in enjoyment. Commuting has become, if not exactly serene, certainly an enjoyable form of relaxation and therapy, a time when I can be in pleasant surroundings considering things that interest me. I find that the shortest distance between two points is not a hotly driven straight line, but rather the route that is the most interesting. (Here, too, this is easy to write, but the change was no less than phenomenal. Now I even wave other drivers into the spot in front of me.)

As my thinking processes were changing, so were some of my bodily practices. Apparently I have had high blood pressure for years without knowing it. This condition was discovered in a routine voluntary health check at work. Other than being twenty-five pounds overweight, I was doing rather well in the examination up to the point of the blood pressure test. The woman administering the test took her readings and then said quietly, "I don't want to worry you, but I think you should have your family doctor check your blood pressure." I acknowledged that that was probably a good idea and said that I would do it sometime. "Mr. Anderson," she said, her face very serious. "Your blood pressure is a little high and you really should see if he can see you this afternoon."

If she had taken another reading at the end of that sentence, I think my blood pressure would have blown the top off the measuring device. "You're serious," I said, and she nodded.

"It isn't at a dangerous level, but you are right on the threshold, and you should take it seriously." That afternoon my doctor confirmed I did indeed have high blood pressure, and he put me on some medicine to control it. It was not an easy thing to do. The doctor kept increasing the dosage until, a year later, I was taking several pills a day to cool down the pipes. It did contain my high blood pressure, but the doctor wasn't pleased with having to introduce so many chemicals into my body to do it.

A few months after Black Sunday, I mentioned to Bob that I felt so relaxed I thought my blood pressure problems might have eased a bit. Bob said that was a possible side effect of how I now viewed myself and the world about me. He suggested two things: that I talk about it with my doctor and that I get an inexpensive device so I could check my blood pressure at home. I did both. The doctor said I could cut back, one capsule at a time, but to measure my blood pressure morning and night and to check with him if it wasn't stable and within a normal range.

Within a week I was off of all medicine, and just this week a doctor who did not know of my previous history of high blood pressure commented very favorably on my current blood pressure. Surely in my case the high blood pressure was a physical reaction to how I thought about myself.

Another, more readily observable physical manifestation of my bad self-concept was my weight. Like a lot of other people, I had seesawed up and down on weight-loss programs of one kind or another. I had finally given them up as a lost cause and accepted the fact that I was and always would be fat. "Fat is where it's at," I would say, eating another helping at dinner.

My weight problem was not specifically addressed in therapy. At most, it may have been mentioned once or twice in passing, but not in any sense in treatment. But to my amazement, and that of my doctor, I began to lose weight. I did, in fact, without trying and with no ongoing consciousness of it, drop twenty pounds. I will never forget the day I walked into my tailor's with all my pants and asked him to take them in two inches.

The predominant characteristic of my entire life before therapy had been the belief that others were superior to me. The drop in my blood pressure and weight further discredited that belief. It affirmed that I am not inferior to others and that I had subconsciously begun to think of and to treat myself in the same way I thought of and treated others. I now found others interesting and even loveable, and that was exactly how I came to accept myself as well. I simply quit being hard on myself. It was a conspicuous leap from one style of life to another. No longer did I curse myself if I made a mistake. I forgave myself, instead. And more and more I found myself doing that with my family and others. I did not look for nor anticipate perfection, and I wasn't disappointed when perfection didn't happen—in me or in others.

There are people who knew the pre-therapy Deacon who may have thought me to be "laid back." If that is so, and I think in some cases it is, it was only because I acted that way as a technique for winning their approval. Today I *am* laid back.

Now, there's a wonderful side benefit to this. I find I can do more than I thought I could. Of course, like all people, some things I do better than other things, some things I do better than other people do them, and some things I do less well than other people do. The thrilling thing is I am doing things which I rarely tried before, or at which I have previously failed. Sometimes I do okay—other times not so great. But win or lose, I enjoy the doing, and I am winning far more often than ever I thought I would.

The most critical relational question going into therapy was, How would it affect my marriage? What would happen if I came back a different person? How would Mary react, and how would a different me react to Mary? Here I had the great good fortune of having a wife who was "with me" without restriction as I went through the therapy process. She understood the nature of the pain, as well as the need for me to relive those incidents which were causing the pain so that the pain itself might be exorcised once for all.

She endured the mood changes that occurred during therapy and those times when I would return from a session torn up by discoveries of my childhood. (Most of the time I left the session with a sense of accomplishment and discovery. Only rarely did I leave as depressed as when I arrived.)

The major change that took place in our relationship was that Mary and I began to talk. We talked about everything. We talked about my early life and about her home life, which had been no more satisfying than mine, and about how as children we had coped with our circumstances. We talked about the early years of our marriage, about our children, and about our future.

As we talked, I found out something very new to me. I found out Mary cares about me. I found out she loves me. We still talk about when she began to love me. But when it began is not important to either of us. What is important is that she loves me now, and I know it.

The quality of our togetherness is rich and tough and growing. We make decisions jointly. In doing this I have developed a new appreciation for Mary and a deeper understanding of my love for her.

That is also true of my children, who are now all adults living nearby. Our aim is to help and encourage them however we reasonably can, but also to let them go. We are not responsible for their decisions. When they make decisions we would not make, we regret it, but it doesn't change our love for them, and they know it. We love them for who they are, not what they do. We do not use our love to manipulate them. It is freely given and freely received, and that is a two-way street.

Therapy virtually revolutionized how I thought about and dealt with my boss—call him Fred. Fred was in critical ways a carbon copy of my dad. He was a driven man who saw life only from his personal vantage point and, unlike Dad, was unscrupulous in his determination to outdo the next guy. He hated *no* for an answer, and some of the supervisors who reported to him were not about to say no. Like him, they would say and do almost anything to advance their careers. I would not lie nor cheat to advance Fred's career, and that brought some inordinate pressures on me.

As I matured through the therapy process, I found myself applying understanding and forgiveness to Fred. The change in my attitude was astounding. I quit seeing Fred as a threat; instead he became an interesting person. Resentment yielded to appreciation, and I came to like being with him, even with all his excesses, which I now accept as frailties. Peering through the cracks in the crust of his ambition, I could see that he did care about people. They had to come second to his ambition, but he cared.

His attitude toward me seemed to change, as well. He became much more friendly and, I think, even trusted me to a degree. And when he left the company, I regretted it and wished him well.

It has been my lifelong habit to reassess what I believe about God as often as new data comes along, whether from the Bible, the newspaper, other people, or elsewhere— such as therapy. My psychological stumbling blocks were not related to faith in God nor to my position as a sinner saved by grace. I had come into therapy believing in God as revealed through Jesus Christ, and that did not change. *I* changed, and that was all for the better.

In retrospect it seems strange that the disconsolate freight of my childhood did not much discolor my faith. To God be the glory and credit for that. The change of my spiritual compass during therapy was subtle. It was more a freshening than anything else. I now came to God with a comfortable objectivity, born of accepting who I am as I am. As I became relaxed in my own presence, it carried over into my relationship with God. I have a stronger appreciation for his efficacious care, for me and for others.

The change was less subtle, however, in how I related to people in the church. Here, too, I no longer held up unreal expectations for them. With my stress level plummeting, I no longer needed to pose as someone different than who I really was. I let me be me, and I let them be them, and the result was a new pleasure in being in the company of believers.

I also became more sensitive to Christians who have distorted perceptions of themselves and the world. I quickly went public about my therapy, not only because I no longer needed to present myself as someone I was not, but also to encourage other believers who were smiling or frowning to cover similar emotional pain to seek help. Some of them sought and got help. Others remain in the closet but are for the first time in their lives wondering if it is okay to seek psychological assistance. Our local church is even planning to add professional counseling to its long list of ministries.

As I cast off the mental baggage of a lifetime, I approached the Bible on a much broader scale and with new enthusiasm. I took up a course of study in the Master of Theology program at New College Berkeley. The result, which is still in process, is a deeper understanding of and appreciation for God's Word.

DR. RICHARD:

Now the fruit of Deacon's persistence and struggle through the therapy process began to appear. As the traumas of early life were revealed and restructured, a deep healing began. Fundamentally, this healing affected how Deacon experienced himself both cognitively and emotionally. He had a new appreciation of himself which he had never before possessed. It was fascinating to see how many areas of his life were affected. I want to look more closely at this because the changes in Deacon are typical of changes that many persons go through when they see psychotherapy to its conclusion.

First, Deacon's parents were humanized. He was able to see them realistically and accept them for who they really were, not who he wanted them to be. *Second, life became much less threatening.* In fact, it became something to be affirmed and enjoyed. His fear of life was gone and with it, behaviors driven by the fear. *Next he observed some genuine changes in his body*—in particular, his blood pressure lowered to the normal range, and his weight dropped to a healthy level.

Then he also found that his relationships with important people in his life improved, particularly with his wife, children, and his boss. Basically he became more open with, and much less critical of, others. Thus he experienced a degree of closeness with others that had eluded him before. *Finally, Deacon developed a profound sense of caring for his own person.* His new self-acceptance, self-understanding, and self-appreciation were evidence that he truly had begun to love himself.

This kind of change revolutionizes a person's life. In a real sense, it feels as if life is starting over. Certainly there is continuity with the old, but the new perspective opens such fresh awareness and new vistas for exploration and development that the old life is cast in shadows; it is still a part of one's history, but it no longer has the powerful hold that it once did. This is true personal liberation, where God helps us break the chains of our debilitating past so we are free to become the person he intends us to be. In the most complete sense, this is what it means to live to our "potential."

Unlike some Christians who complete psychotherapy, Deacon experienced no major changes in his perception of God. His belief system did not alter, but he did become more comfortable in his faith. As he became more accepting of himself, he was able to have a less fluctuating awareness of God's acceptance.

I have often observed that Christians in therapy change their perceptions of God, especially those who have had a particularly critical parent and/or who were brought up with a theological dogma excessively focused on sin and God's judgment. Usually a perception shifts from one of a wrathful and judgmental God to one of a more accepting, affirming, and caring God—an image which is much more balanced and congruent with the God of the New Testament as revealed through Jesus Christ.

Never in all my experience of treating Christian clients has anyone stated that his or her faith was somehow diminished. To the contrary, their experience has been like Deacon's, or even more positive, as their emerging wholeness allows them to experience God at a level of understanding that was not available to them before.

After observing these changes in people, it seems very natural to conclude that our perception of God and our relationship with him are indeed influenced by our patterns of thinking, feeling, and behaving toward ourselves and others. While we may intellectually assent to certain beliefs, it is clear that full realization of what those beliefs can mean in our lives may be blocked by psychological baggage that must first be dealt with. Only then can we realize all that God has for us. This is precisely why effective psychotherapy is, in its most profound sense, a spiritual as well as a psychological journey.

The spiritual and psychological are inextricably interwoven in the human being. Treating one dimension always affects the other. Just as psychotherapy brings some changes in faith, so does a religious conversion experience often bring significant changes in psychological functioning. To the Christian psychotherapist, the interfacing of the spiritual and psychological represents a fascinating intersection which, in my judgment, cannot be avoided if the whole person is to be treated.

In Deacon's case, psychotherapy brought about changes that affected the primary manifestation of his faith—his church life. He began living with a new authenticity in the church, became even more motivated to grow in his faith, and developed a strong desire to help others who are bogged down in a psychological quagmire. He was now, in a very exciting way, beginning to move *toward* people rather than away from them.

ANDERSON:

Conclusional Dreaming

As I explained earlier, all of my life I had dreamed that I was enroute to some place which was never quite defined. Just as I thought I was about to reach my destination, I would find that there were additional and more complicated obstacles to overcome; finally there would be an obstacle so great that I could not think of a way to cross it. It was my responsibility in the dream to get to the destination, and I never made it. The outcome was that I would awaken in the morning to face the new day already fatigued from the struggle in the dream. Six months to the day after Black Sunday, I had a dream which revisited old, familiar territory.

This was a terror dream. I was at home with Mary when the telephone rang. I answered and heard the voice of a very elderly Swedish woman who said, "I am very old"—and something to the effect that she was helpless.

Then a gruff male voice came on the line, and I heard him say they were now going to burn the old lady's hand very badly. I somehow knew they intended to press her hand on the burner of a stove and that they weren't making an idle threat. They really intended to carry it out.

There was within the dream the implication that I had some responsibility for saving the old lady, that there was something I could do, but nothing specified what it was.

I listened for a moment while the torture arrangements were still going on and then quietly hung up the phone. I decided since there was nothing I could do about it, it really wasn't my problem nor my responsibility. It was too bad, but I was not involved.

I wrote the above account the next morning. Then I followed it with my interpretation of the dream.

I was both the old lady and myself. The phone call represented pressures exterior to me and which had no claim on me, trying to load guilt on me and responsibilities which are not really mine, and I rejected them, just as I am learning to do in life.

Those pressures probably represent the programming I once accepted, that I was supposed to be responsible for the things people indicated in one way or another I was responsible for, but I no longer will let those patterns take control of my life. I control my life now.

This account from my journal gives an insight into how my thought processes had changed. One of the things I was thinking, but that I didn't get down properly on paper, was that the old Swedish woman probably reflected how my childhood environment framed the way I thought about myself and the world about me. In other words, I thought about things in the ways I was taught to think about things.

The old thought patterns challenged my new determination to remain independent of them as I faced myself and the world. My new ways of thinking allowed me to realize that, as in the old terror dreams, there could be no resolution of the problem by trying to work it out according to the old game rules; I would never get to my destination, never succeed, never wake up rested.

This dream was in a very real sense a revised version of the shootout at the OK Corral. The bad guys, represented by the gruff male voice, would stoop to anything to keep their advantage. That included an appeal to conscience. But even as I listened to them, I realized that this was their game, not mine. It was a fabricated idea of guilt they were playing on, not any actual guilt.

Two important concluding signals stand out. In the dream, *I "quietly hung up the phone."* I did not wake up to consider reentering the dream to alter it to end in a new way. I disconnected the call. It was a deliberate act of closure. I was done with the old ways and would no longer entertain them, even in my dreams.

The second and even more inspiring indication of conclusion appears in the last sentence of my interpretation of the dream. "I control my life now," I wrote. Had I said it out loud, I would have said, *"I control my life now."* No longer do the ghosts of times past determine how I will react to life as I find it. I'll handle it, thanks, and I'll do a better job than they ever did.

DR. RICHARD:

Really . . . could it be said better? No further comment is needed.

VI.

FOREVER

**The joy of ever un-
folding newness**

You turned my wailing into dancing;
   you removed my sackcloth and
    clothed me with joy,
that my heart may sing to you and not
   be silent.
   O Lord, my God, I will give you thanks
   forever.

                    —Psalm 30:11–12, NIV

ANDERSON:

David bursts forth in irrepressible praise for what God has
done for him. His testimony sets the strings of my heart vi-
brating in glorious response. My own experience is all there
in David's psalm—the misery, the regret, and the mourning
followed then by redemption, relief, and celebration.

I cannot "be silent. O Lord, my God, I will give you
thanks forever." Thanks be to God.

Thanks, too, to Bob Richard who labors for the Lord in
the vineyard of man's thought processes.

What God did for me through Bob's intervention in my
hopeless way of thinking and what Christ did for me on the

cross are certainly not equivalent—there is no equivalence to the cross—but in both instances I find myself saying, "I was lost, but now I'm found. I was blind, but now I see."

Intervention was the key for me, both in salvation and in turning from confused thinking to orderly thinking. When I was unable to extract myself from the quicksand of tortured thinking, God in his grace injected himself and got me to solid ground. Bob was God's available instrument for reaching out to grasp my outstretched hand. With his help the death spiral of my thinking was finally broken. And I am free at last!

As the old tapes of wrong perceptions fade away, what about the road ahead?

New tapes are being created—tapes of hope and interest and curiosity and confidence. A pattern of growth has taken root, a casual blend of optimism balanced by a realistic appreciation for myself and for others. The future has taken on a lovely soft glow.

DR. RICHARD:

Effective psychotherapy, as in Deacon's case, changes some of the fundamental ways in which we approach life. It creates a new set of understandings and emotional responses which allow an individual to proceed through life in a far more healthy and emotionally satisfying manner. However, it must be stressed that while effective psychotherapy brings about the necessary internal changes in the human psyche, many behaviors have been practiced for so long that they seem to have developed a life of their own (much like an unwanted habit). In some instances, the skills necessary to substitute a more effective behavior for an old, ineffectual one simply have not been developed. Thus, in the days following the intense internal work, there usually are sessions focused on creating new behavioral responses which are supported by the new internal changes.

Take, for example, the matter of becoming more assertive. Being assertive is, simply stated, having the ability to respond appropriately and clearly to a situation where one feels treated unfairly. Persons with low self-esteem often have a great deal of difficulty being assertive, since they basically believe that their rights are not as important or as valuable as someone else's. Since they are not assertive, they have never developed the skills necessary to act assertively. Even though their self-esteem may grow significantly in the therapy process, they still need to learn how to engage in effective assertive action and to practice such behavior.

Thus Deacon and I worked together as he experimented with new ways of relating and behaving which he had either never tried or had tried but with considerable frustration. One area that was particularly interesting was painting. For years Deacon had been frustrated with not being able to get forms which were visualized in his mind put down on the canvas in a way that satisfied him. However, at this point in his therapy he was able to free himself utterly of some unrealistic artistic expectations and began to experiment with new colors and more easily flowing forms, which have brought him great satisfaction. I have seen one of these paintings, and it is truly beautiful.

Psychological and spiritual development continues and need not ever stop during a lifetime. Genuine psychotherapy clears away the impediments of our past that may at worst lead us down the path to our own destruction or at least sidetrack us from a healthy and full development. But the choice to really do something about those impediments remains ours and ours alone. No value is derived from simply blaming our past, but the detrimental effects of the past in us can be healed if we are willing to risk engaging in the work it takes to see ourselves through.

After Words

ANDERSON:

There aren't many good things about breaking a leg, but at least the incident is self-proclaiming. The cast and crutches signal the world that you are not presently able to perform certain tasks everyone else finds routine.

The person with thinking problems often has no visible injury. There is no cast he may wear that announces damage in his ability to cope with the circumstances which are handled routinely by his peers. He looks normal. He may act like anyone else. He may be so good at acting normal that no one has any idea that he is in pain. Yet the hurt he suffers is terrifyingly real. He would surely give anything to merely suffer the pain felt by the person with a compound fracture of the leg. That is a pain one gets over.

His smile may be a defense mechanism to disarm persons and to keep them from becoming aware of his feelings of inadequacy. His smile may be a survival technique, masking the on-going agony of mislearned thinking. But inside he understands there is no vacation from mislearned thinking.

I think it is the emotional pain, as much as the errant thinking, which makes a mental hurt so pervasive. Like a bad infection, a mental hurt spreads its poison through all of the emotions, thought processes, and belief systems.

It has not been easy nor a pleasure to sift through material I don't care to remember. But sift through it I have, and here I am, still in the light of day and still celebrating God's goodness to me.

You were the motivation for this book. It is my prayer that something in my experience gives you hope, particularly if you are unable to make sense out of the world, unable to understand why things are as they are—why you are as you are, unable to account for a good God in the face of personal struggles and tragedy. Like me, you might be unable even to find a real purpose for being.

If that describes you, I know where you're coming from. I also know that many people cannot rescue themselves from the dilemmas of such intense personal struggles. But here's good news: God can use psychotherapy to bring healing and psychological resurrection.

I fully intend to spend the rest of my life in celebration of my new resurrection. I hope you will join me.

DR. RICHARD:

Over the course of this account, I have deliberately tried to refrain from interjecting some of my own feelings about the therapy process as I experienced it. I felt that to relate my subjective reactions could be confusing and detract from a clear unfolding of Deacon's journey.

However, with every client's journey the psychotherapist also makes a journey. As a human being, I cannot escape my own feelings and reactions to my clients' difficulties, struggles, and ultimate resolution or nonresolution of whatever brought them into my office in the first place. For me, the psychotherapeutic journey is always full of challenge, new insights, and the possibility of the great and deep satisfaction of seeing a human being go through some life-changing psychological transformations. However, the journey can also have its share of frustrations, problems, and dry spells—which can be very draining mentally and emotionally.

As I began my work with Deacon, I found myself becoming highly motivated to assist this bright, articulate man in extricating himself from his psychological prison. Deacon's own determination to get beyond his stultified life certainly was a strong encouragement to me as I labored along with him. Early on, I was aware of Deacon's commitment to do something about his life, albeit he did not know what to do.

Such commitment gave me early assurance that I could help him because I knew I could provide some answers about what needed to be done. As we moved through the therapy process, I observed patterns emerging which are consistently associated with positive change, and these patterns served to reassure me that the direction of our work together was correct.

The psychotherapeutic journey is not unlike taking a voyage in a small boat. One is continually checking on the course and evaluating conditions and making new decisions as conditions change. During the therapy process, as new data comes to light, as denied experiences are disclosed, one must continually reevaluate the meaning of these revelations as they bear on the direction of therapy and on the kind of interventions which will be of maximum assistance in achieving the agreed upon treatment goals. This can be demanding work.

Obviously I do not see the effective psychotherapist as simply a passive listener. To the contrary, he or she is an active and involved listener who shares equally with the client the responsibility for bringing psychotherapy to a successful outcome.

Without a doubt, the most intense part of Deacon's therapy, both for him and for me, was the series of sessions involving regression and restructuring. During regression, emotionally charged material can come out in waves, flooding the office atmosphere. Yet I must remain sufficiently detached to carefully guide the regression and restructuring work. At no time can I become inundated with a client's traumas, or overwhelmed by his or her struggle.

As a client's pain begins to subside, as old hurts are healed, as new and more effective ways of being and living in the world begin to emerge, I feel a kind of thrill—an excitement and satisfaction which cannot be duplicated in any other area of my life. Certainly I experienced these feelings with Deacon, and I shared them with him as our work progressed.

There is a final word I wish to add here. I have always viewed my professional work as a form of Christian ministry. I have always been aware that God's Spirit is every bit as present in the consultation room as it is beyond the confines of those four walls. I have always been aware that God is the author and preserver of life whether it be physical, mental, or spiritual, and that he is at work in the world bringing about healing and reconciliation. I see my work as part of this healing and reconciliation process.

Deacon has begun a new life, a gift from God to him and to me as well. I rejoice with him, and I know that in his journey to mental wholeness my own journey as a psychotherapist and human being has been immeasurably enriched. To be part of a magnificent change process in another person's life is truly a privilege for which I am profoundly grateful.